Choose LOVE

Print ISBN 978-1-63609-714-5

Published by Barbour Publishing, Inc., 1810 Barbour Drive, Uhrichsville, Ohio 44683, www.barbourbooks.com

Our mission is to inspire the world with the life-changing message of the Bible.

Printed in China.

3-MINUTE DEVOTIONS FOR TEEN GIRLS

CAREY SCOTT

Introduction

Here's a collection of thoughts to help you focus on God's greatest command, which is to love. We're not only to love the Lord but also others. What does that look like? How do we know if we're loving in the right ways? Let's see what God's Word has to say! Within these pages you'll be guided through just-right-sized readings that you can experience in as few as three minutes:

Minute 1: Reflect on God's Word.
Minute 2: Read real-life application and encouragement.
Minute 3: Pray.

These devotions aren't meant to be a replacement for digging deep into the scriptures or for personal, in-depth quiet time. Instead, consider them a perfect jump start to help you form a habit of spending time with God every day. Or add them to the time you're already spending with Him. Why not share these moments with friends, family, classmates, and others? Chances are they're looking to better understand God's command to love too.

Your words are a flashlight to light the path ahead of me and keep me from stumbling.

Psalm 119:105 TLB

Let Love Prevail

Let love prevail in your life, words, and actions.
1 CORINTHIANS 16:14 VOICE

The Bible is very clear about God's call for us to love. You can find this unwavering command woven throughout its pages from Genesis to Revelation. And because it's important to God, it should also be important to us.

When scripture says to let love prevail, it means it should be the top priority in how we choose to live. With our family, with our friends, and even with strangers, love should be what guides our words and action. We should choose it over any other feeling or emotion. And friend, that takes strength from the Lord to walk out.

Before your feet hit the ground in the morning, ask God to give you the desire and ability to let love reign in your heart. It doesn't mean you won't experience anger or frustration at others, but it means you'll lead with love as you work through challenges and disagreements.

LORD, LET LOVE PREVAIL IN HOW I LIVE MY LIFE EACH DAY. HELP ME CHOOSE TO LOVE IN EVERY SITUATION. ESPECIALLY WHEN IT'S HARD TO DO. AMEN.

What Love Is

Love is patient; love is kind. Love isn't envious, doesn't boast, brag, or strut about. There's no arrogance in love; it's never rude, crude, or indecent—it's not self-absorbed.

1 CORINTHIANS 13:4–5 VOICE

Sometimes we get confused about what love *is*. . .and what it is *not*. Rather than look to God's Word to define it, we tweak it to fit our circumstances. We weaponize love, placing unrealistic expectations on others. We let it be what justifies our harsh responses or bad-mannered actions. And it looks nothing like it's supposed to.

But God tells us exactly what love looks like in the life of a believer. It's patient rather than annoyed. Kind rather than cruel. Love doesn't envy but celebrates instead. It's not proud, mean-spirited, or crude. And it's focused on others.

When you choose to love this way, it glorifies God, benefits you, and blesses those in your life.

LORD, I CONFESS THE TIMES I'VE NOT LOVED OTHERS YOUR WAY. STARTING TODAY, I WANT TO DO BETTER! HELP ME REMEMBER WHAT LOVE IS AND WHAT IT IS NOT. AND LET ME BE MINDFUL OF IT IN EVERY RELATIONSHIP. AMEN.

Love in Truth

Love isn't easily upset. Love doesn't
tally wrongs or celebrate injustice;
but truth—yes, truth—is love's delight!
1 CORINTHIANS 13:5–6 VOICE

Love that stays focused on truth strengthens the bonds we feel with one another. It builds trust between friends and those who fill our hearts. It grows deeper roots in our families because love is reinforced on the regular. And as we focus on grace and compassion, love has the opportunity to bloom in beautiful ways.

But the reality is that it's hard to love others while keeping truth in view. It takes God's help because there are so many factors that can mess us up. For example, when we feel anxious or insecure in relationships, we're more willing to entertain joy-stealing lies. Fear often keeps us tangled and unable to believe motives. And when we feel worried about how things will work out, we're more apt to keep score as we judge one another.

Every day, ask God to let you thrive in relationships by loving in truth.

LORD, KEEP MY HEART PURE AND HOPEFUL
FOR THOSE I CARE ABOUT. HELP ME CHOOSE
GRACE SO MY RELATIONSHIPS GROW. AMEN.

Choosing Love over Resentment

Love puts up with anything and everything that comes along; it trusts, hopes, and endures no matter what.
1 Corinthians 13:7 VOICE

Don't let today's verse signal that abusive behavior is okay with God. Choosing love doesn't mean you're a doormat so people can walk all over you. You don't have to allow harmful treatment from friends or boyfriends. Teachers, coaches, employers, church leaders, and everyone else in authority don't get a free pass to be cruel or insulting either. Consider that you are choosing love by setting up appropriate boundaries to keep you physically and emotionally safe, while keeping your heart from becoming bitter. You can trust and hope in God, and He'll give you the strength to endure the hard seasons, even if from a safe distance.

When you live unoffended by the wrongdoings of others, it keeps you from the prison of unforgiveness. You're not condoning bad behavior. Instead, you are clinging closely to the one who will protect and sustain you. You're choosing love over resentment.

LORD, GIVE ME THE GRACE TO CHOOSE LOVE WHEN SOME ARE UNLOVABLE AND THE WISDOM TO KNOW WHEN BOUNDARIES ARE NECESSARY. AMEN.

Love Goes on Forever

All the special gifts and powers from God will someday come to an end, but love goes on forever. Someday prophecy and speaking in unknown languages and special knowledge—these gifts will disappear.

1 CORINTHIANS 13:8 TLB

What a great reminder that love will last forever. There is nothing that can stop it from infiltrating the lives of those who follow the Lord. It's seared into our DNA, unable to die away. While everything else will eventually fade away—including the gifts and powers that come from God to our earthly lives—love never will.

Friend, what is the Holy Spirit speaking into your heart right now? Is love alive and active, or are you allowing bitterness to take root? Are hard moments and difficult people robbing you of warm and fuzzy feelings in other areas? Are you losing joy for this life, sinking into the pit of despair?

Let God reignite the love that's faded. God says it will go on forever, so ask Him to make it so!

LORD, LOVE FEELS FAINT THESE DAYS. HELP IT BURN BRIGHT IN ME ONCE AGAIN. AMEN.

Extraordinary Love

"This is how much God loved the world: He gave his Son, his one and only Son. And this is why: so that no one need be destroyed; by believing in him, anyone can have a whole and lasting life."

JOHN 3:16 MSG

Can you imagine the grit it took for God to give up His Son to death on a cross? He watched as Christ suffered. God saw the persecution. He witnessed the injustices that came His way. And because God chose love, His one and only Son, Jesus, stepped out of heaven and into the world to save us. Now that is love, friend. That is how much God values you.

Today, meditate on that sacrificial decision of compassion for us. Talk to the Lord, sharing your gratitude. Express your thankful heart for His willingness to choose love on your behalf. What a beautiful example of selflessness we can show others by how we treat them.

Let's choose to love in extraordinary ways too. With God's help, we can let others know how much they matter through the words we share and the actions we take.

LORD, HELP ME SHOW OTHERS EXTRAORDINARY LOVE. AMEN.

Being Kind and Loving

But if a person isn't loving and kind, it shows that he doesn't know God—for God is love.

1 John 4:8 TLB

Whoa. This is a big scriptural statement! It tells us that how we treat others reveals our heart for God. It uncovers the truth of our faith. And it's a fantastic reminder that because God *is* love, we have access to a deep well of it to lavish on others. Are you choosing to do so?

Every day we get to decide how we will act toward others. We get to determine how we treat our parents, our siblings, our friends, our teachers, our teammates, and those we meet on the street. We can be kind, or we can be mean. We can be loving, or we can be hateful. It's our choice. But because we know God and follow His ways, we can ask for help so we're a blessing to those around us. We can choose to be kind and loving, even when it feels impossible.

LORD, HELP MY ACTIONS TOWARD OTHERS REFLECT MY FAITH. AMEN.

Showing Deep Love

Most important of all, continue to show deep love for each other, for love makes up for many of your faults.

1 PETER 4:8 TLB

How can we show deep love to others? Maybe it's obeying your parents when your heart's desire is set on something else. Maybe it's spending time with a sibling, making them a priority in your busy schedule. Maybe it's being a respectful student to your teachers, even if everyone else is being dismissive. Or maybe it's befriending the new kid who is struggling to fit in.

Be intentional to be the kind of girl who cares about the feelings of others. Take the time to choose to love in a world that doesn't seem to do that well anymore. Through your faith, you have the power to make a difference in the lives of others by simply showing compassion and care. Be the one who decides to live that way.

LORD, FORGIVE ME FOR THE TIMES I'VE NOT SHOWN DEEP LOVE TOWARD OTHERS. STARTING TODAY, OPEN MY EYES AND HEART TO THE IDEA OF EMBRACING THE POWER OF LOVE TO THOSE AROUND ME. AMEN.

New Wardrobe

So, chosen by God for this new life of love, dress in the wardrobe God picked out for you: compassion, kindness, humility, quiet strength, discipline.

COLOSSIANS 3:12 MSG

Have you considered there's a wardrobe change of sorts once you accept Jesus as your personal Savior, believing Him to be God's one and only Son? When you become a believer, there is a supernatural change that happens. It's a change of heart that manifests as a change of behavior. And it's wonderful.

Where you used to be snarky and selfish, you're now more compassionate. Kindness comes out more often than harsh responses. There's a humility that makes you approachable. And rather than react in hurtful ways, you're able to take a breath and be loving. Your relationship with God changes everything. And it's only through His power and grace that this kind of change is possible.

LORD, THANK YOU FOR MY NEW WARDROBE OF COMPASSION, KINDNESS. HUMILITY. AND STRENGTH. HELP ME CHOOSE TO WALK THROUGHOUT MY DAY PROUDLY WEARING IT. LET EVERY WORD AND ACTION REFLECT THE CHANGES YOU'VE MADE IN MY LIFE.

The Command to Forgive

Be even-tempered, content with second place, quick to forgive an offense. Forgive as quickly and completely as the Master forgave you.

Colossians 3:13 msg

One of the hardest ways we're told to love others is by forgiving them. We can be kind in the moment. We're able to smile or hug for a second or two. But sometimes, the thought of extending grace to someone who's deeply hurt us feels close to impossible. We don't want to let them off the hook for the pain they've caused. We don't want them to avoid the natural consequences of their actions. So, we hold on to the offense.

Friend, this is a struggle we all face. Forgiving is hard, no matter how you slice it. But God commands it of His followers. He wants us to choose love over holding a grudge. Compassion over getting even. And when you can't seem to bring yourself to forgive, ask God to change your heart.

LORD, I WANT TO BE QUICK TO FORGIVE SO NOTHING KEEPS ME FROM CHOOSING LOVE. FILL ME WITH GRACE FOR MY FRIENDS AND FAMILY. AMEN.

Putting on Love

And regardless of what else you put on, wear love. It's your basic, all-purpose garment. Never be without it.

Colossians 3:14 MSG

Sometimes to change a behavior, muster courage, or find focus, it helps us to have a visual. Before a free throw in basketball, some people see the ball swish the net before they shoot. Before the hard conversation with a teacher, some will visualize a successful result play out in their mind first. Maybe you've done the same in your life at times. Choosing to love is no different.

What if before your feet hit the ground in the morning, you imagine putting on love like an oversized coat? It engulfs your body in abundance. Then as you go through your day and face challenging people, you can choose to love because there's so much to give. In those moments when you're faced with being kind or being dismissive, the decision is easier to make. In God's eyes, choosing love matters greatly!

LORD, I UNDERSTAND THE VALUE OF WEARING LOVE. HELP ME PUT IT ON EACH DAY SO I CAN TREAT OTHERS WITH KINDNESS AND COMPASSION. AMEN.

Supporting Friends

"I demand that you love each other as much as I love you. And here is how to measure it— the greatest love is shown when a person lays down his life for his friends."

JOHN 15:12–13 TLB

What are some ways you can support your friends sacrificially? Maybe you help them work through a tough class in school. Maybe you help them navigate a difficult situation at home. Maybe you help meet their basic needs by sharing your resources or connecting them with someone who can intervene. Or maybe you stand up for them, advocating when they feel weak or overwhelmed. By doing so, you are choosing love.

Ask God to open your eyes to the needs of those around you, because sometimes they are hard to see. Life gets busy. You have your own struggles to manage. And rather than see what others may need, we get focused on ourselves instead.

LORD, I CARE FOR MY FRIENDS. AND I DON'T WANT TO BE SELF-ABSORBED WHEN THEY NEED MY HELP. LET ME BE AWARE AND SENSITIVE TO THEM. READY TO LOVE BIG AT A MOMENT'S NOTICE. AMEN.

But Love Is the Greatest

*But now faith, hope, and love remain;
these three virtues must characterize
our lives. The greatest of these is love.*
1 CORINTHIANS 13:13 VOICE

Friend, what characterizes your life? How would people describe you? It matters to God because He is crystal clear on what should set you apart from unbelievers. And because it matters to Him, it should matter to us too.

Our *faith* should stand out in how we act and what we say. It ought to be obvious to others that we value following God's commands and trust His leading, even when it's hard to do. In addition, *hope* should define our attitude. When life gets messy, our outlook should be expectant as we trust God to show up. But most of all—more than anything else—*love* should be what characterizes us. In every relationship and in all circumstances, He wants us to lead with it. God wants you to choose love every time.

LORD, LET FAITH, HOPE, AND LOVE BE WHAT
DEFINES MY LIFE. HELP ME REFLECT THESE TO
MY FRIENDS AND FAMILY EVERY DAY. AMEN.

The Command to Love

"So I give you a new command: Love each other deeply and fully. Remember the ways that I have loved you, and demonstrate your love for others in those same ways."

JOHN 13:34 VOICE

In His Word, God talks often about the command to love. It's not a mere suggestion but a deep desire for His followers. Because of the love lavished on us. . .we're to expend love on others with similar passion and purpose. How are you doing with that?

Are you showing love to your parents, even when they drive you nuts? Are you being kind to your siblings, giving them time and attention on the regular? When at school or on the court, are you respectful to your teachers and coaches? Do you show compassion to those who need a friend or advocate? Are you devoted to being thoughtful toward others—especially the ones who may not agree with you? At every chance, choose to love in ways that will bless others and glorify the Lord.

LORD, LET MY HEART ALWAYS BE BENT TOWARD LOVING OTHERS DEEPLY AND FULLY. AMEN.

Actions Speak Louder

"This is how everyone will know that you are my disciples, when you love each other."

JOHN 13:35 CEB

Actions matter more than words. You can tell someone you love them, but when the heat is turned up in their life, do you show them love? Do you reach out in support? Do you rally around them in compassion? Do you find ways to meet their immediate and pressing needs? Our words don't matter if our actions don't match them.

The Word says that people will know we love God by how we love others. The ways we treat those around us will reveal our faith. And the more time you spend deepening your relationship with the Lord through prayer, time in the Bible, and meditating on scripture, the more love will become your default response in life. When that happens, your actions will point to God in heaven. Choosing love reveals your heart for the Lord and following His ways.

LORD, HELP ME LIVE IN SUCH A WAY THAT MY FRIENDS AND FAMILY KNOW I AM A CHRIST FOLLOWER. LET MY ACTIONS AND WORDS OF LOVE ALIGN IN WONDERFUL WAYS. AMEN.

Because God First Loved Us

We, though, are going to love—love and be loved.
First we were loved, now we love. He loved us first.

1 JOHN 4:19 MSG

Your ability and desire to love is because you were first loved by God. He introduced you to the feeling. He made it come alive in your heart. God is the one who showered you with His goodness, helping you understand what compassion and care look like. And because love has bloomed in you, you're able to pass it along.

That's why you can muster kindness to siblings that drive you nuts. It's why you can forgive and ask for forgiveness from friends. Love is why you can't stay mad at your parents when they discipline. And it's why your heart is full of empathy and concern for those who are hurting. So keep choosing love, friend. You can access it anytime. The world needs God's love flowing through you toward others.

LORD, THANK YOU FOR LOVING ME FIRST AND GIVING ME THE PERFECT EXAMPLE OF WHAT IT LOOKS LIKE. WITH YOUR DIVINE HELP, I WANT TO ALWAYS CHOOSE TO LOVE OTHERS. AMEN.

Don't Hate

Those who say, "I love God" and hate their brothers or sisters are liars. After all, those who don't love their brothers or sisters whom they have seen can hardly love God whom they have not seen!

1 John 4:20 CEB

If you're able to love God with all your heart but hate those around you—even if it feels justified—let it be a red flag. There may be those who you deeply disagree with. Maybe someone hurt you in significant ways. You may struggle to connect with offensive people, mean-spirited in what they do or say. And there may be differences too big to overcome. But the Lord doesn't see the justification in hating them.

Rather than take that strong stance, spend time with God. Ask Him to help you set appropriate and healthy boundaries to keep you emotionally safe. Commit to pray for your enemies, asking Him to let you see them through His eyes. Choosing to love and not curse keeps your heart from becoming hard and bitter. And it proves your love for God is authentic.

LORD, HELP ME LOVE OTHERS NO MATTER WHAT. AMEN.

Unselfish Love

And this commandment we have from Him, that the one who loves God should also [unselfishly] love his brother and seek the best for him.

1 JOHN 4:21 AMP

If God commands you to love unselfishly, then rest assured He will give you the ability to do so. As mere humans, we're incapable of it. Alone, it's impossible. But when you ask the Lord to fill your heart with generosity toward others, He will. When you ask for kindness to be your default button, it will happen. And when faced with a difficult situation and you ask God to help you be selfless as you navigate it, He will bless you.

So often we think it's all up to us. We put pressure on ourselves to be the perfect Christian girl who always responds with grace and love. Talk about pressure! But when we realize grace and love come from God above, it brings freedom from our unrealistic expectations. While we still must choose love, He is the one who gives us the ability.

LORD, HELP ME LOVE OTHERS UNSELFISHLY BY FILLING ME WITH THE DESIRE AND DIVINE POWER TO DO SO. AMEN.

But Love Covers

Hatred stirs up strife, but love covers and overwhelms all transgressions [forgiving and overlooking another's faults].

PROVERBS 10:12 AMP

God's desire is for us to forgive others rather than hold on to our hurt or anger. Even more, we're called to overlook their faults because we love them. It's deciding our relationship means more than holding a grudge. It's choosing to cut someone a break for being imperfect. It's letting them off the hook for making mistakes. It's allowing grace to flow freely, covering the wrongdoing with love instead. And it takes God's help.

Today, tell God about your struggles with this. Talk to Him about the friends, family, teachers, coaches, and coworkers who make forgiving hard to do. Ask for a greater measure of compassion to offset the anger that often invades your heart and mind. And ask for the strength to choose love over unforgiveness so you can live in peace with others.

LORD, IT'S HARD TO OVERLOOK THE HURT AND FRUSTRATION THAT OTHERS CAUSE. IT'S HARD TO LET LOVE SPEAK LOUDER. SO PLEASE GIVE ME THE DESIRE AND ABILITY TO FOLLOW YOUR COMMAND. AMEN.

With All You Have

Jesus said, "The first in importance is, 'Listen, Israel: The Lord your God is one; so love the Lord God with all your passion and prayer and intelligence and energy.' "

MARK 12:29–30 MSG

As believers, we should choose to love God with all we have. It's an intentional decision to focus our life on loving and honoring Him in meaningful ways. It isn't easy to do, but Jesus says it is important. How are you doing with that?

How do you love God with your passion? Do you let His Word burn in your heart and let it flow into your day from there? Are you loving the Lord through prayer, talking with Him regularly about anything and everything? Do you meditate on scripture, finding ways to let its wisdom help you choose wisely? And do you give your relationship with God concentrated time, energy, and connection?

Friend, when you choose to love God with all you have, it will bless you and glorify Him. And it will help you live and love those around you with passion and purpose too.

LORD, HELP ME LOVE YOU WITH ALL I AM. . .EVERY DAY. AMEN.

Love Others the Same

The second great commandment is this: "Love others in the same way you love yourself." There are no commandments more important than these.

MARK 12:31 VOICE

What are some of the ways you are kind to yourself? Chances are you do things that make you feel good, like eat well, exercise, and get plenty of sleep. Maybe you buy yourself items that delight your heart. Do you set aside downtime if necessary or pack your days if you're more of an extrovert? Do you make sure your basic needs are met each day? Friend, how do you love yourself?

The Lord says the time and attention we take to be good to ourselves should also be taken to be good toward others. It's His desire for you to love those around you, like you love yourself. It's not necessarily in the exact same ways, but in your heart and motive. It's a call to not put yourself above others. It's choosing to love them with the same passion and purpose. And even more, it's God's command.

LORD, HELP ME CHOOSE TO LOVE OTHERS LIKE I LOVE MYSELF. LET MY HEART ALWAYS BE FOR THEM. AMEN.

No Fear of God

We need have no fear of someone who loves us perfectly; his perfect love for us eliminates all dread of what he might do to us. If we are afraid, it is for fear of what he might do to us and shows that we are not fully convinced that he really loves us.

1 John 4:18 TLB

At every turn, God chooses love. While He has every right and reason to punish, the Lord loves us perfectly. That doesn't mean we'll be saved from the natural consequences of our sins. He won't make life easy and pain-free. And we will face challenging seasons with friends and family. But in His great love, He will be there to help us walk through the difficulties ahead.

When you mess up, go right to God. There's no reason to be afraid of His wrath, because we can be confident in His love. We can be convinced we're fully accepted. And we can choose to embrace this truth every day.

LORD, THANK YOU FOR BEING A SAFE PLACE WHERE I'M LOVED PERFECTLY! AMEN.

Practice Loving Others

Dear friends, let us practice loving each other, for love comes from God and those who are loving and kind show that they are the children of God, and that they are getting to know him better.

1 John 4:7 TLB

The closer you become to God, the better you love those around you. You will have more compassion for the hurting. You'll have more patience for the kids you babysit. You will care about others' feelings and act accordingly. You will model respect in the classroom and on the court. You won't be perfect, but you will be purposeful to love others well.

When you get the chance, practice loving one another. It may be messy at times. You may fail miserably. There may even be those who require every bit of your strength to show care and concern. But as you choose love, it will come easier. And it will reveal God's work in your life and in your heart.

LORD, LET MY RELATIONSHIP WITH YOU BE EVIDENT IN HOW I TREAT THOSE AROUND ME. AND HELP ME ALWAYS PRACTICE LOVING OTHERS IN WORD AND DEED. AMEN.

Tangible Ways

But think about this: while we were wasting our lives in sin, God revealed His powerful love to us in a tangible display—the Anointed One died for us.

Romans 5:8 voice

God showed His love for you in a very tangible way through His Son's death on the cross. Even while we were stuck in a cycle of sin, God's love was burning brightly for us. So much so that He made a way to bridge the gap sin left by sacrificing Jesus. Absolutely amazing!

Today, we can choose to show love in tangible ways too. We can be the Lord's hands and feet in the world—an extension of His goodness and compassion toward others. What are some ways you can show love to those around you? How can you bless your teachers, coaches, small group leaders, friends, neighbors, and family? Ask God to help you demonstrate love in wonderful and meaningful ways, and then choose to delight each person's heart with purpose.

LORD, THANK YOU FOR THE TANGIBLE DISPLAY OF LOVE THROUGH JESUS. HELP ME FIND TANGIBLE WAYS TO EXPRESS COMPASSION AND KINDNESS TOO! AMEN.

Loving God

"Sir, which is the most important command in the laws of Moses?" Jesus replied, " 'Love the Lord your God with all your heart, soul, and mind.' This is the first and greatest commandment."

MATTHEW 22:36–38 TLB

Every day you have a choice to love God or ignore Him. You can invite Him into your hectic schedule or push through on your own. It's up to you.

How can you love the Lord with your heart, soul, and mind? Let Him be a constant companion as you navigate your day. Talk to Him about frustrating people. . .challenging moments. . .irritating situations . . .and discouraging news. But also share what excites you and brings joy. Tell God about your hopes and dreams. Ask for wisdom or peace when you need it. Let Him be involved in it all. When you choose to love Him in these ways, you'll be fulfilling the greatest command.

LORD, I'M INVITING YOU TO BE PART OF MY DAY. IN EVERY WAY. LET MY HEART AND MIND BE TURNED TOWARD YOU AS I CHOOSE TO LOVE YOU WITH INTENTIONALITY. AMEN.

Loving Others

"The second most important is similar:
'Love your neighbor as much as you love yourself.'"
MATTHEW 22:39 TLB

Yesterday we learned the greatest commandment is to love God with your heart, soul, and mind. Today, we read that the second most important command is to love your neighbor (love others) in the same measure as you love yourself. While neither is easy, both are important as believers.

Loving is a choice we must make. Sometimes it's a no-brainer because certain people matter greatly to us. Even when we argue or they make us mad, our feelings for them are deep and never waiver. But other times, loving feels almost impossible. It's hard to have compassion for those who have hurt you or someone you care about. When they are mean-spirited and look for ways to make you feel insignificant, how can we love?

Ask God for help. He knows every detail and will meet you in the struggle. Today, trust Him to make ways for you to choose love.

LORD, THIS COMMAND FEELS HARD. ESPECIALLY WHEN IT COMES TO CERTAIN PEOPLE. HELP ME CHOOSE LOVE ANYWAY. AMEN.

Being Patient with Others

Be humble and gentle. Be patient with each other, making allowance for each other's faults because of your love. Try always to be led along together by the Holy Spirit and so be at peace with one another.

EPHESIANS 4:2–3 TLB

When we are patient with others, it's an act of love. Every time we refuse to sit in judgment when they fail, we are loving them. God wants us to live peacefully with those around us, and we can't make that happen if we're critical. We can't be reckless with how we treat others. Instead, the Lord tells us to be humble and gentle.

Community is important to God, and He wants us to handle one another with care. His plan is for peace. So ask Him to help you be full of kindness and compassion, especially when you're struggling to be that way. Ask for perspective so you can choose love even when it's difficult. And trust God to align your heart for others with His.

LORD, HELP ME CHOOSE TO LOVE OTHERS WELL BY BEING PATIENT, HUMBLE, AND GENTLE. AMEN.

Loving through Obedience

"If you love me, show it by doing what I've told you. I will talk to the Father, and he'll provide you another Friend so that you will always have someone with you. This Friend is the Spirit of Truth."

JOHN 14:15 MSG

When we obey God, it reveals our heart. Choosing to do what He asks shows that we love Him over our own fleshly desires. Just like it does for our parents, following His rules speaks volumes by showing we care about what's important. And it's honoring.

While we may try to, obeying often takes divine intervention. Our humanity kicks in and we get rebellious from time to time. We want to do things our own way and on our own timeline. And because God knew our needs, He sent the Holy Spirit. As our friend, He's the one who enables us to obey. The Spirit is a constant companion who will always bring truth. And with His help, we can choose to love God through obedience.

LORD, THANK YOU FOR THE HOLY SPIRIT WHO EMPOWERS ME TO LOVE YOU THROUGH OBEDIENCE. AMEN.

The Gift of True Friends

A true friend loves regardless of the situation,
and a real brother exists to share the tough times.
PROVERBS 17:17 VOICE

What a gift to be a true friend and to have a true friend. Sometimes they are the ones we lean on the most to walk us through the hard times. They're often our secret keepers, heart protectors, problem solvers, and soul sisters. And we know we can depend on their love and kindness, regardless of the situation we find ourselves wading through.

Who are your true friends? Who are you a true friend for? Take a moment to thank God for these gifts, as scripture says all good things come from above. Because He loves you, these kinds of friends have been handpicked. Some for this season and others for a lifetime. But they make a difference in our lives in deep and meaningful ways.

If you don't have them yet, pray them into your life! Tell God your need, and wait for Him to bring them at the right time.

LORD, THANK YOU FOR THE GIFT OF TRUE FRIENDS. HELP ME BE ONE TOO! AMEN.

You Are His Child

See how very much our heavenly Father loves us, for he allows us to be called his children—think of it—and we really are! But since most people don't know God, naturally they don't understand that we are his children.

1 JOHN 3:1 TLB

God chose you! Out of His great love, the Lord has fully embraced you as His child. Even with all your flaws—with every shortcoming and imperfection—you're allowed to be called a child of the Most High. Regardless of the ugly moments when you screamed at your siblings, were rude to your parents, or betrayed a friend, you are deeply loved. And there is nothing that can change it.

Friend, you have the ability to choose God every day too. A *yes* to spending time in prayer, reading His Word, meditating on scripture, listening to a sermon, or soaking in worship music allows you to reciprocate His love in meaningful ways. The intentionality of those decisions delights God's heart. They speak loudly about your faith. And they draw you closer to the Father.

LORD, I LOVE BEING CALLED YOUR CHILD. HELP ME LOVE YOU BACK! AMEN.

Seeing the Fruit

So if we stay close to him, obedient to him, we won't be sinning either; but as for those who keep on sinning, they should realize this: They sin because they have never really known him or become his.

1 JOHN 3:6 TLB

This scripture is a very strong warning for everyone who calls themselves a believer. When we accept Jesus as God's Son and our personal Savior, there should be a heart transformation. Our lives should look and feel different. We should want to abandon our old self—our sinful and selfish ways—and instead embrace a new life in Christ.

As we stay close to God and obey the commands we find in the Bible, recognize this decision is a beautiful act of love. We're choosing to grow in our faith by following Him. What God finds important, we do too. What He wants for our life, we do as well. But if we aren't changing our focus from self to Savior, let it be a red flag. Did we really choose to love God with our whole heart?

LORD, LET ME SEE THE FRUIT THAT COMES FROM A GENUINE RELATIONSHIP WITH YOU. AMEN.

Showing Love

So now we can tell who is a child of God and who belongs to Satan. Whoever is living a life of sin and doesn't love his brother shows that he is not in God's family; for the message to us from the beginning has been that we should love one another.

1 JOHN 3:10–11 TLB

When you choose to hold on to unforgiveness rather than choose to love others, it is telling. Each time we hold a grudge against a friend, refuse to forgive a parent, hate a teacher or coach, stay angry at a sibling, or let offenses rule our day, it reveals the state of our heart. The Lord is crystal clear in His command to love one another. As a matter of fact, it's the second greatest command He makes.

Let's be women who choose to love, even when it takes all we have. Let's decide that nothing trumps God's charge to show care and compassion to those around us. And let's remember that selfishness is a sin. With His help, we can learn to embrace His will over our own. We can choose to love.

LORD, HELP ME SHOW LOVE. . .ALWAYS. AMEN.

Laying Down Our Life

We know what real love is from Christ's example in dying for us. And so we also ought to lay down our lives for our Christian brothers.

1 JOHN 3:16 TLB

This is a call for us to be inconvenienced for the sake of others. To *lay down our lives*—while it can mean exactly what it says—also means to put others before you. It means being the hands and feet of Jesus to those who need help. It's bringing His hope to the hopeless. How can you do that in your community, in the classroom, in a church, at a job, or on the court? Ask God to show you, and then watch for opportunities to present themselves.

Maybe it's volunteering your time. Maybe it's befriending the outcast. Maybe it's donating to a shelter. Or it may be tangibly meeting the needs of those you know or love. Today, ask God to use you in extraordinary ways. By doing this, you're choosing to love just as the scriptures say. And it's a powerful expression of God's work in your heart.

LORD, USE ME TO BLESS OTHERS. AMEN.

Actions and Words Align

Little children, let us stop just saying we love people; let us really love them, and show it by our actions.

1 John 3:18 TLB

Actions always speak louder than words. Think about it. You can tell your little brother you love him, but will you show it when he frustrates you? Will you be kind to your beloved coach when she pulls you from the court? Will your friendship stay intact when your bestie makes a mistake that hurts you?

The truth is it's easy to tell someone you love them. Those words can flow freely and often. But when a relationship faces difficulties and discouragements, will you choose to let your actions convey the same love? Let's make sure how we act aligns with what we say. And when it's a struggle, let's ask God for help so we can be consistent for those we care about.

LORD, I CONFESS THE TIMES MY WORDS AND ACTIONS HAVE NOT ALIGNED. HELP ME LOVE OTHERS CONSISTENTLY IN WHAT I SAY AND IN WHAT I DO SO NO DOUBTS ARISE IN THEIR HEARTS. AMEN.

Believe and Love

*And this is what God says we must do:
Believe on the name of his Son Jesus
Christ, and love one another.*

1 John 3:23 TLB

What are the ways you show love and kindness toward others? Maybe you pay attention in class when your teacher is speaking. Maybe you are verbally affirming to the new youth leader at church. Maybe you spend quality time with your grandparents regularly. Maybe you cook a meal or clean around the house without being asked. Or maybe you find intentional ways to show appreciation to those around you.

These acts of kindness come from a heart invested in a relationship with the Lord. It's from Him that we're able to love others selflessly. He gives us the desire to choose compassionate ways to bless those we care for. And the time we spend deepening our faith creates a softening inside, leading us toward feelings of love.

LORD, I DO BELIEVE IN YOU. AND I KNOW IT'S WHY I AM ABLE TO LOVE OTHERS WITH FERVOR. LET IT ALWAYS BE SO. AMEN.

Owing Others Love

Don't owe anyone anything, with the exception of love to one another—that is a debt which never ends—because the person who loves others has fulfilled the law.

ROMANS 13:8 VOICE

Consider that the Lord wants you to owe nothing but love to others. It's not a joy-draining demand but a life-giving command that brings blessings to all involved. Even more, it's not a one-and-done concept. Instead, God wants us to see it as an ongoing effort. It should be our pleasure and passion to love others well.

Is it always easy to do? No, ma'am. Often, it takes grit and grace we can only get from the Lord. Does it come easily? Sometimes, yes! But other times loving others is a choice. In those moments, we must decide to show kindness and compassion to the unlovable with a pure heart. And with God's strength, we can do it.

LORD, SHIFT MY HEART AND MIND TO UNDERSTAND THE VALUE IN LOVING OTHERS CONSISTENTLY. IT'S NOT ONLY A COMMAND BUT ALSO A PRIVILEGE. AND I WILL CHOOSE EVERY DAY TO LOVE IN YOUR STRENGTH. AMEN.

The Law of Love

Love does no wrong to anyone. That's why it fully satisfies all of God's requirements. It is the only law you need.

Romans 13:10 TLB

The Word of God says the only law we need is the law to love. Think about that for a moment, considering how that choice impacts every relationship in your life.

When you choose to love your parents, you obey their rules without complaining. When you choose to love your friends, you celebrate their accomplishments rather than be jealous of them. By choosing to love your teammates and coaches, time off the court and on the bench doesn't upset you. Loving others means not participating in gossip. It means being generous with your time. It's being cooperative rather than complaining. And it informs how you respond, making sure you're showing compassion and care in the right moments.

Be the kind of young woman who does no wrong to anyone. This isn't a call to be perfect but to be purposeful in how you treat others.

LORD, HELP ME CHOOSE TO LOVE OTHERS WELL. GIVE ME THE ABILITY TO FOLLOW THIS POWERFUL LAW, EVEN WHEN IT FEELS IMPOSSIBLE TO DO SO. AMEN.

A Beautiful By-Product

We know how much God loves us because we have felt his love and because we believe him when he tells us that he loves us dearly. God is love, and anyone who lives in love is living with God and God is living in him.

1 JOHN 4:16 TLB

Simply put, love is a beautiful by-product of being a true believer of Jesus. We read about God's deep love for us in the Bible. We feel His love in our life as we supernaturally receive what we need to navigate each situation. And God shows us of His love as we experience His goodness in each day, regardless of our circumstances. Because He is love, it's an unavoidable blessing and gift. That means we can access it whenever we need it.

Ask God to help you choose to love others in meaningful ways. Give them your time. Speak kind words. Be willing to help. Listen when they need it. Pray when asked. Show compassion and give care without hesitation.

LORD, THANK YOU FOR BEING LOVE BECAUSE IT ALLOWS ME TO SHOW IT TO OTHERS. YOU THINK OF EVERYTHING. AMEN.

Don't Pretend to Love

Don't just pretend that you love others:
really love them. Hate what is wrong.
Stand on the side of the good.
ROMANS 12:9 TLB

Chances are you know what it feels like when others pretend to care about you. You've probably experienced fake love from people you thought were friends, only to later discover how they really felt. And when you did, it just felt lousy.

God wants us to choose to really, truly love others instead. What might that look like in your life? Remember that He's looking for authenticity not driven by dishonest and selfish motives. He wants us to steer clear of what is wrong and align ourselves with what is good. We're to love those around us in meaningful ways that bless them and glorify God. And at every opportunity, we're to exercise compassion and kindness toward others. How are you doing with that?

LORD, HELP ME SHOW FAITHFUL LOVE. HELP ME BE GENUINE. DEPENDABLE. AND WHENEVER I COME TO A CROSSROADS OF OPTIONS. LET ME CHOOSE TO STAND ON THE SIDE OF GOOD AND LOVE OTHERS WELL. AMEN.

Satisfied with God's Ways

Don't copy the behavior and customs of this world, but be a new and different person with a fresh newness in all you do and think. Then you will learn from your own experience how his ways will really satisfy you.

ROMANS 12:2 TLB

Be a breath of fresh air to those around you. Rather than fall in line with what the world says is right or wrong, let God transform your heart to be a new creation who follows His way. Be a young woman who stands up for truth and advocates for others. Speak with kindness, but don't be a doormat. Treat everyone with respect. Be willing to listen first before you feel the need to speak. And remain resolved to stand firm in God's commands for your life without caving to peer pressure. This is choosing love—love for the Lord, love for yourself, and love for others.

While some may tell you differently, God's ways are satisfying. Live them out and see for yourself.

LORD, HELP ME FIND A FRESH NEWNESS BY FOLLOWING YOUR WILL AND WAYS. LET MY HEART BE SATISFIED BY YOU ALONE. AMEN.

Working Together as One

Just as there are many parts to our bodies,
so it is with Christ's body. We are all parts of it,
and it takes every one of us to make it complete,
for we each have different work to do. So we belong
to each other, and each needs all the others.

ROMANS 12:4–5 TLB

The truth is we need one another. God made us to be in community with a variety of other believers because we fit together to further His kingdom. An assortment of family and friends as well as a mixture of other people are important parts of your life and work together as one. Each brings different talents and skills that support the bigger picture of faith. And together, we are a force for goodness.

This is why we choose to love others. We need to be together in Christ! We can't stay in self-protection mode because we've been hurt by community in the past. It leaves a noticeable gap. So choose to embrace others and the collective God has designed for you to thrive in.

LORD, THANK YOU FOR THE GIFT OF MY COMMUNITY. EVERY DAY, LET ME CHOOSE IT. AMEN.

With Brotherly Affection

Love each other with brotherly affection and take delight in honoring each other.

ROMANS 12:10 TLB

When scripture tells us to love with brotherly affection, it means with deep warmth. This is a notable kindness and sympathy we extend. There's intentional care and compassion in our actions. Our words are affirming in meaningful ways, bringing hope and encouragement when times are trying. And it's often how we feel about our family and close friends.

Chances are, we'd agree there are times this is simpler to walk out than others. Some people are just easier to love. Regardless, God's Word is clear that we're to choose to love other believers even when it's challenging. Even more, we are to delight in it rather than doing so begrudgingly. Ask God to tender your heart so brotherly affection comes quickly and without stress. And then watch as He blesses your obedience and boosts their sense of significance.

LORD, SOMETIMES LOVING OTHERS IS THE HARDEST CHOICE TO MAKE. WOULD YOU HELP ME DO SO THROUGH YOUR STRENGTH, ALLOWING ME TO FOLLOW THIS COMMAND WITH PURPOSE? AMEN.

Praying for Offenders

If someone mistreats you because you are a Christian, don't curse him; pray that God will bless him.

ROMANS 12:14 TLB

Whoa! Sometimes we read scriptures that are hard to digest, and other times we read ones that feel impossible to walk out. For some, today's verse may feel that way in spades because it's asking us to pray for those who hurt us. When we've been wounded for being a believer, praying for God to bless the one who offended us usually isn't our default response. But friend, ask God to make it become just that.

Pray for the friend who mocks your faith. Pray for the boss who treats you badly for requesting Sundays off for church. Pray for the brother who picks on you relentlessly for reading the Bible. Pray for peers who make fun of you for praying before eating at lunchtime. Pray for the teammate who laughs because you listen to worship music rather than what's trendy. By doing this, you're choosing to love the unlovable. And God sees it.

LORD, PLEASE STRENGTHEN ME TO FOLLOW YOUR COMMAND TO PRAY FOR MY OFFENDERS. AMEN.

Meeting in the Moment

When others are happy, be happy with them.
If they are sad, share their sorrow.
ROMANS 12:15 TLB

One important way you can choose to love others is to meet them in the moment. Whether it's a sad or happy situation, just being present sends a powerful message that they matter to you. Don't be afraid to share their sorrow—instead be willing to sit in it with them. And when there's reason to celebrate, be quick to rejoice with them too! What a privilege to be part of another's life in such ways.

Who in your group of friends needs your support right now? Is there a family member who could use some cheering on? Do you know of someone needing to be championed as they take the next step? Embrace every opportunity to connect with others in meaningful ways. God created community for believers, and it's important to not only enjoy it but also contribute as well. Ask Him to open your eyes and ears to see and hear the needs of those around you. And then step out in faith, linking arms in beautiful and mighty moments.

LORD, HELP ME MEET OTHERS IN THEIR MOMENTS. AMEN.

Confident in Community

Work happily together. Don't try to act big. Don't try to get into the good graces of important people, but enjoy the company of ordinary folks. And don't think you know it all!

ROMANS 12:16 TLB

Humility is important to God. Scripture says that it's pride that goes before the fall, so we need to stay grounded in the truth of who we are. . .and who we are not. When we embrace who God created us to be, we're choosing to love ourselves. Not in a prideful way but in a grateful way. We're letting Him know we like our skills and talents. It's saying we appreciate the gifts baked into us. And it's recognizing that we were made on purpose and for a purpose.

Friend, let confidence guide you into community. Be happy to bring your God-given abilities and hard-earned areas of expertise to the group. Be willing to work with others, not concerned about status or popularity. And recognize all that others bring into the mix too. This is a recipe for working happily together, and it delights God's heart.

LORD, HELP ME CHOOSE TO LOVE MYSELF SO I'M CONFIDENT AND NOT CONCEITED. AMEN.

Loving through Tough Conversations

Never pay back evil for evil. Do things in such a way that everyone can see you are honest clear through.

ROMANS 12:17 TLB

If you're committed to choosing love, then there is no place for revenge. There's no room for dishonesty. Because anything that hurts another isn't motivated by genuine compassion, pure and simple. In your opinion, there may be justification for your anger. There may be a well-concocted strategy to hide your true motivation. But love is kind and doesn't dishonor others. It keeps no records of wrong nor does it delight in evil. Instead, it rejoices in the truth.

Friend, love others enough to be honest. If they've hurt you or treated you poorly, talk about it with them. Share your feelings. Explain how their actions frustrated you. Care enough to try and work through disagreements, believing they want the same. Sometimes choosing to love others means you have tough conversations in hope of reconciliation.

LORD, THANK YOU FOR REMINDING ME THAT HONEST CONVERSATIONS OVER VENGEFUL PLANS REVEAL MY LOVE FOR THOSE IN MY LIFE. AMEN.

God's Heart for Harmony

Don't quarrel with anyone. Be at peace with everyone, just as much as possible.

Romans 12:18 TLB

Having fights and disagreements with people is a normal part of life. We each have our own ideas and opinions about how to move forward. And like everyone else, we feel confident our ways are the best ways. So how could we not quarrel from time to time? We are imperfect people, living in an imperfect world, with other imperfect people. There's no way around it.

The challenge is to balance our irritation with a desire for peace. It doesn't mean we stuff feelings, but maybe we don't have to be offended at every turn either. What if we asked God to help us know when to share our frustrations and when to let them go? And what if we asked for a heart bent toward peaceful resolutions rather than exasperated exchanges? We need the Lord's help to love family and friends well. We need His help to seek harmony with classmates, teammates, and coworkers. Friend, we need God's heart for harmony every day.

LORD, GIVE ME A DESIRE TO BE AT PEACE AS MUCH AS POSSIBLE. AMEN.

Let God Handle It

Dear friends, never avenge yourselves. Leave that to God, for he has said that he will repay those who deserve it. Don't take the law into your own hands.

ROMANS 12:19 TLB

God is very clear in His Word when He says for us to *not* take matters into our own hands. Plotting and planning revenge isn't for us to do. Your heavenly Father will manage in His own way and in His own time. So, when someone deserves a rebuke, He promises to handle it. Friend, don't you see this as freedom?

Trusting God in these situations gives us breathing room. It's not up to us to figure out! We can choose love over retaliation. Compassion rather than vengeance. Kindness and not payback. And when you think about it, wouldn't you rather someone have to answer to the Lord over you anyway?

LORD, THANK YOU FOR BEING MY PROTECTOR AND THE ONE TO AVENGE ON MY BEHALF. HELP ME KEEP THIS PERSPECTIVE WHEN SOMEONE HURTS ME IN ANY WAY. I CHOOSE TO LOVE THEM AND TRUST YOU. AMEN.

Being Full of Compassion

Instead, feed your enemy if he is hungry. If he is thirsty give him something to drink and you will be "heaping coals of fire on his head." In other words, he will feel ashamed of himself for what he has done to you.

ROMANS 12:20 TLB

The perfect response when someone is treating you badly is to be kind. In a world where you can be anything, be full of compassion. You don't have to treat others the way they treat you, especially when it's awful. Instead, you can be the one to respond with a generous spirit. You can choose love.

This doesn't mean you're a weak person who can't stand up for themselves. You're not being a doormat for others to walk all over. Instead, you're choosing to see the bigger picture. You're being the bigger person. And when you don't respond in kind, it gives God the opportunity to move in the heart of the one being hurtful to you. And He will honor your thoughtful choice.

LORD, PLEASE STRENGTHEN ME TO CHOOSE LOVE WHEN IT FEELS HARD TO DO. AMEN.

Conquering Evil with Kindness

Don't let evil get the upper hand,
but conquer evil by doing good.
ROMANS 12:21 TLB

Did you know that when you do good in the world, it helps conquer evil? In some situations, it may even help shut it down completely. When the new girl at school is treated poorly and feels unaccepted, your friendship changes everything. When your classmates treat the substitute teacher with disrespect, but you show intentional kindness, it makes a difference in her day. Every time you refuse to gossip, evil loses. When you lead your team with compassion rather than cruelty, evil is shut down.

Today, ask God to open your eyes to see where you can conquer evil through goodness. Where can you shine Jesus into the world? How can you bring encouragement in bighearted ways? What friend or family member needs to be lavished with your love and support? Ask God to open your eyes to opportunities to defeat evil with kindness.

LORD, EQUIP ME TO BRING YOUR GOODNESS INTO THE LIVES OF THOSE AROUND ME SO EVIL LOSES ITS POWER. AMEN.

Even When at Our Worst

"I tell you, love your enemies. Help and give without expecting a return. You'll never—I promise—regret it. Live out this God-created identity the way our Father lives toward us, generously and graciously, even when we're at our worst. Our Father is kind; you be kind."

LUKE 6:35–36 MSG

Scripture tells us that being *at our worst* is no excuse for bad behavior. That means we can't scream at our siblings for hogging the bathroom when we're running late, or be rude to a teammate for missing the shot that would've won the game. Waking up cranky doesn't give us a free pass to be dismissive to our parents. And a bad test grade doesn't justify being rude to the teacher.

Instead—no matter how we feel—God wants us to live generously. He wants us to be gracious in our responses. We're to help and give, even to those we're in conflict with. And kindness should be our DEFAULT button. Yes, friend, the Lord wants us to choose love without fail.

LORD, THERE IS NO EXCUSE FOR TREATING OTHERS BADLY. HELP ME ALWAYS CHOOSE LOVE. AMEN.

Being Bold Anyway

When people hate you, when they exclude you and insult you and write you off as evil on account of the Son of Man, you are blessed.

LUKE 6:22 VOICE

Don't be shy about your faith. Instead, boldly walk it out without apology. Offer to pray for someone who's hurting. Thank God before you eat your lunch. Be willing to tell your testimony when the opportunity arises. Share powerful scriptures with others. Blare worship music when you feel like it. Choose to love those around you, just as God commands. And if people treat you badly for it, know you are blessed.

There will be times your faith offends people. They won't like what you stand for and may be vocal about it. They may even alienate you, trying to make you feel alone and unloved. Let this only strengthen you through the Lord because you're able to see the bigger picture. The truth is you're fully and completely loved, so let compassion flow out.

LORD, GIVE ME THE COURAGE I NEED TO SHINE YOUR LIGHT FOR OTHERS TO SEE, EVEN IF THEY RESPOND IN HATEFUL WAYS. AMEN.

Keep Loving Them

If you're listening, here's My message: Keep loving your enemies no matter what they do. Keep doing good to those who hate you. Keep speaking blessings on those who curse you. Keep praying for those who mistreat you.

LUKE 6:27–28 VOICE

Today's verses are echoing a command that's mentioned several times in the Word. God is clear when He tells us to love our enemies regardless of what they do. If they hate you, love them. If they treat you like dirt, love them. If they turn others against you, love them. If they ruin your reputation or damage your relationships, love them. If their words are full of profanity toward you, love them. Even more, pray for them.

Friend, this is a hard path to walk unless you are clinging to God for strength and might. Only through Him can you find the confidence needed to stand strong no matter what. Cry out to the Lord and watch as He blesses your obedience.

LORD, COME CLOSE TO ME AND STRENGTHEN ME TO LOVE MY ENEMIES NO MATTER WHAT THEY DO. I'M DESPERATE FOR YOUR HELP. AMEN.

Do for Others

Think of the kindness you wish others would show you; do the same for them.

LUKE 6:31 VOICE

Take a minute to consider how you'd like others to treat you. Maybe you want to feel like you're good enough. Maybe you want to have a sense of belonging. Do you want genuine friendships, ones where you always have each other's back? Do you want others to appreciate your quirkiness? Maybe you want a second chance to try again or the gift of forgiveness. Or maybe you want friends who will call you higher and point you to the Lord. What would make your list?

Scripture says we should be intentional to treat others the way we want to be treated. It's not being manipulative, and it's not interacting with wrong motives. Instead, it's choosing to love others in ways that are important to you. It's blessing others in the ways you want to be blessed. And even if it's not returned, let there be satisfaction in knowing you are obeying God's command and that doesn't go unseen.

LORD, HELP ME TREAT OTHERS THE WAY I WANT TO BE TREATED WHILE KEEPING PURE MOTIVES. AMEN.

The Challenge to Love the Unlovable

Listen, what's the big deal if you love people who already love you? Even scoundrels do that much! So what if you do good to those who do good to you? Even scoundrels do that much!

Luke 6:32–33 VOICE

It's hard to love those we consider unlovable. People who are rude, classmates who bully, teammates who only care about themselves, family members who won't listen, and coworkers who blame us for their faults—these are the ones who challenge our willingness to be compassionate. Their lack of concern often makes us feel the same toward them. And the distance between our hearts and theirs widens.

The call for love and kindness is hard at times because we don't get it in return, and it hurts our feelings. It hardens our hearts toward them. And it makes us want to turn away and give attention to those who love us back. Ask God to give you the desire and ability to love the unlovable. He will.

LORD, HELP ME LOVE EVERYONE. NOT JUST THE ONES WHO MAKE IT EASY. AMEN.

Choosing Love over All Else

If you don't want to be judged, don't judge. If you don't want to be condemned, don't condemn. If you want to be forgiven, forgive.

LUKE 6:37 VOICE

We can't expect others to treat us in certain ways if we're not willing to do so for them. Relationships are a give-and-take adventure, and they require sacrificial love to make them work. If we won't extend grace, how can we ask for it? If we won't assume the best in them, we can't expect it back. If we don't tame our tongue, then we shouldn't hope they do.

Relationships thrive the best when we choose love over all else. Why? Because love covers a multitude of sins. It allows us to overlook shortcomings and frustrations. Since our heart for them is always good, we can accept imperfections rather than always point them out. How are you doing with this? Are you being the kind of friend you want? Are you being a positive family member?

LORD, HELP ME DO BETTER. LET LOVE GUIDE HOW I TREAT THOSE I CARE FOR. AMEN.

Love Lavishly

Don't hold back—give freely, and you'll have plenty poured back into your lap—a good measure, pressed down, shaken together, brimming over. You'll receive in the same measure you give.

Luke 6:38 voice

Choose to love lavishly! Scripture says to not hold back, because your measure of compassion and kindness shown toward others will be returned. . .and then some. As a believer, you have every incentive to be generous. You have the freedom to love others with over-the-top abundance. And when you open your heart and pour out His goodness, God will return it to you.

Where can you love big today? In your circle of friends and family, who needs a good dose of thoughtfulness? In what ways can you bless someone with kindheartedness? Ask the Lord to open your eyes to how to be His hands and feet in the world. Let Him lead you to love.

LORD, HELP ME WANT TO LOVE EXTRAVAGANTLY. GIVE ME THE DESIRE TO BE EXCESSIVE IN HOW I BLESS OTHERS. LET ME SHOW COMPASSION IN MEANINGFUL WAYS. AND LET ME DO THIS IN YOUR NAME ALWAYS! AMEN.

Produce Good Things

It's the same with people. A person full of goodness in his heart produces good things; a person with an evil reservoir in his heart pours out evil things. The heart overflows in the words a person speaks; your words reveal what's within your heart.

LUKE 6:45 VOICE

If you have genuine love for someone, scriptures say goodness will automatically flow from you in abundance. Your life will produce good things! That love will make you honor the rules set forth by your parents. It will allow you to be honest and full of integrity in the classroom and on the court. It will make you into a great friend who protects others. You will show kindness to your siblings. Simply put, it will help you care about what matters to the Lord. And through your words and actions, it will show others (and God) the condition of your heart.

LORD, CREATE IN ME A HEART FULL OF YOUR GOODNESS SO I CAN CHOOSE TO LOVE OTHERS WITH IT. LET WHAT I SAY AND WHAT I DO POINT BACK TO MY FAITH IN YOU. LET MY LIFE PRODUCE GOOD THINGS. AMEN.

Loving Because He Lives in You

I have been crucified with Christ: and I myself no longer live, but Christ lives in me. And the real life I now have within this body is a result of my trusting in the Son of God, who loved me and gave himself for me.

GALATIANS 2:20 TLB

As believers, we're to surrender our fleshly desires every day and choose to trust God's will and ways instead. Christ is alive and active in us because we have new life through salvation. That means we have the power—His power—flowing through our veins, giving us the ability to love others with passion and purpose.

Friend, you are not weak anymore. You don't have to let your sinful nature win. And when you want to walk away in frustration, you have the strength to stay. If God is asking you to choose love, with His help and guidance you can do it. Through His strength, you're able to extend grace to those friends and family who get on your last nerve. Trust God and ask Him to make it so.

LORD, THANK YOU FOR NEW LIFE THROUGH YOU. AMEN.

Nothing

I'm convinced that nothing can separate us from God's love in Christ Jesus our Lord: not death or life, not angels or rulers, not present things or future things, not powers or height or depth, or any other thing that is created.

ROMANS 8:38–39 CEB

Do you ever feel like you've let God down because you struggle to love as He commands? Do you worry He is angry about it? Are there times you're afraid He may turn His heart from you? If so, let today's passage of scripture settle your heart.

While choosing to love others is the second greatest command next to loving God Himself, the truth is that failing to do so doesn't separate you from His love. We are imperfect creatures at best. And you may want to show kindness and compassion but often struggle in the moment. Even then, you can rest assured that your failures won't ever disconnect you from the Lord. You are His. . .forever.

LORD, MY DESIRE IS TO LOVE OTHERS WELL. BUT WHEN I FAIL. THANKS FOR PROMISING TO ALWAYS LOVE ME! AMEN.

God's Extraordinary Love

In the same way, the Spirit comes to help our weakness. We don't know what we should pray, but the Spirit himself pleads our case with unexpressed groans.

Romans 8:26 CEB

At every turn, God chooses to love us in the most extraordinary ways. There is nothing He won't do for those who love Him through faith. Today's verse tells us that even when we're tongue-tied, the Spirit deciphers each incoherent prayer for us. When we're too upset and unable to find the right words, our needs are shared perfectly through the Spirit. And when we can't pray at all, God understands the complexity of our situation with complete clarity.

It's hard to comprehend the depth of His love. Our minds cannot fully grasp the ins and outs of God's goodness. But we can know with certainty that He chooses to love us without fail every day and will continue through eternity.

LORD, I APPRECIATE THAT YOU THINK OF EVERYTHING. EVEN IN MY LACKING, YOU INTERVENE IN THE MOST AMAZING WAYS. THANK YOU FOR BEING THE GOD OF EVERYTHING! AMEN.

God Works It All Together

And we know [with great confidence] that God [who is deeply concerned about us] causes all things to work together [as a plan] for good for those who love God, to those who are called according to His plan and purpose.

Romans 8:28 AMP

When you become a believer—accepting Jesus as your personal savior—it's an intentional choice to love the Lord and follow His ways. It's deciding to trust His perfect plan for your life, even knowing you'll walk it out imperfectly. It's understanding that God will use the mountaintop moments and dark valley experiences to help shape you into the woman He planned for you to be. And it's a choice to seek His guidance as you navigate life each day.

God chose to love you, friend. Now you have the choice to love Him as you trust His leading. When you do, you'll be able to see the miraculous way God works everything together for your good and His glory.

LORD, THANK YOU FOR NOT WASTING ANYTHING LIFE THROWS MY WAY. I TRUST YOU TO WORK IT ALL TOGETHER! AMEN.

God's Love Lasts Forever

"Understand, therefore, that the Lord your God is the faithful God who for a thousand generations keeps his promises and constantly loves those who love him and who obey his commands."

DEUTERONOMY 7:9 TLB

Friendships will come and go, maybe even those you thought would last forever. Boyfriends too. Relationships with family members may ebb and flow over time as well. The truth is that your circle of trust will most certainly change as you go through life. And as normal as it may be, it's often difficult because we care for these people deeply. We chose to love them. But few things earthly. . .last.

Scripture is clear, however, that God's faithfulness is unceasing. His love for those who obey His commands lasts forever. And His promises are good for generations to come. He chose you, friend. In a world full of uncertainty, choose to love the everlasting God too.

LORD, THANK YOU FOR BEING A SWEET AND POWERFUL CONSTANT IN MY LIFE. THANK YOU FOR LOVING ME WITHOUT END. EVERY DAY, MY HEART WILL CHOOSE YOU. AMEN.

Make No Mention

"The LORD your God is in your midst, a Warrior who saves. He will rejoice over you with joy; He will be quiet in His love [making no mention of your past sins], He will rejoice over you with shouts of joy."

ZEPHANIAH 3:17 AMP

Just as God promises to make no mention of your past sins, you can choose to love those around you in the same way. Your efforts won't be perfect, but they will be purposeful. The truth is there's no room for scorekeeping in relationships. There's no space for condemnation. Choosing to sit in judgment rather than stand in love will only end up ruining a good thing.

The best way to love others is to follow God's lead. In what ways can you rejoice over those around you? How can you bring joy into your community? Where can you extend grace rather than hold on to offenses? And when you make the deliberate decision to love with purpose and passion—being kind and generous whenever possible—you will watch as your relationships begin to blossom with goodness. Always choose love.

LORD, HELP ME LOVE OTHERS AS YOU LOVE ME. AMEN.

Keeping Short Accounts

Overlook an offense and bond a friendship;
fasten on to a slight and—good-bye, friend!

PROVERBS 17:9 MSG

No matter how much we try to love our friends well, chances are we will hurt them at times. Our heart for them may be full of love, but we are flawed in our humanity. And just as we're poised to hurt them, the same is true on their end. Even in their best efforts, they will mess up too. But we need friends, so how do we protect our hearts?

Today's verse tells us how by offering a powerful way to thrive in community. If we want to love others well, then we must choose to overlook offenses. Forgiveness keeps our hearts from scorekeeping. It allows us to operate in compassion instead. And being merciful adds a level of depth to relationships because it tells the other person they're valuable. When they reciprocate, it speaks the same message to you.

Ask God to help you keep short accounts. As you choose to love in this way, it creates a beautiful bond that's hard to break.

LORD, HELP ME KEEP SHORT ACCOUNTS. AMEN.

Loyalty and Kindness

Never tire of loyalty and kindness. Hold these virtues tightly. Write them deep within your heart.

PROVERBS 3:3 TLB

Done right—with God's strength and might—we can live a life marked by kindness. We can be loyal to those we care about. Whether it's toward a parent, a sibling, a friend, a classmate, a teammate, or a boss, we can choose to show love through our words and actions. We can bring joy to their lives in wonderful ways. We can encourage in hard moments. And we can be the one who points them to the Lord in difficulties.

Today, ask God to write this approach to loving others on your heart so it becomes the operating system you live by. Let it sink deep into your DNA so it develops into a DEFAULT button. He wants you to hold tight to these virtues and walk them out as you navigate relationships. And with His help, you can choose this wonderful way of loving those around you.

LORD, EVEN WHEN IT FEELS HARD. TEACH ME TO ALWAYS SHOW LOYALTY AND KINDNESS. AMEN.

Trust God over Yourself

If you want favor with both God and man, and a reputation for good judgment and common sense, then trust the Lord completely; don't ever trust yourself.

PROVERBS 3:4–5 TLB

We get ourselves into trouble when we trust ourselves over God. When we decide our way is better, or we don't ask Him for wisdom along the way, it's the perfect setup to make mistakes. It's when we say the wrong things in the heat of the moment. It's when we jump to conclusions that aren't correct. It's when we make decisions that end up hurting others. And it's when we are reckless in how we respond to messy moments.

But with God's help, we can choose to love our friends and family by showing good judgment in how we treat those we care the most about. We need His guidance because we are imperfect. We make mistakes even when we think we're doing good. Let's be young women who seek God and trust Him to show us the way.

LORD, I'M A HOT MESS WITHOUT YOU. SHINE FAVOR AND GUIDE ME SO I TREAT OTHERS WITH LOVE. AMEN.

Putting God First

In everything you do, put God first, and he will direct you and crown your efforts with success.

PROVERBS 3:6 TLB

When scripture tells us to put God first in everything, it means we should follow His will and ways over our own. We should ask Him for guidance and wisdom rather than relying on ourselves. We should make sure our choices don't conflict with what God's Word says. And when we put God first, He will show us the path to walk, and He will bless our obedience.

When you're working to be a good friend or trying to figure out life after high school graduation or looking for the right job, put God first. This is choosing to love the Lord with all your heart and mind. As a believer, this is how you surrender in faith. And if you're looking to be successful in life, seeking His plan for your circumstances helps make that a reality.

LORD, I'M CHOOSING TO LOVE YOU BY PUTTING YOU FIRST IN EVERYTHING I DO. FROM THE SMALL DECISIONS TO THE BIG ONES, I WANT WHAT YOU WANT FOR ME. PLEASE SHOW ME THE WAY. AMEN.

The Holy Spirit

The Holy Spirit produces a different kind of fruit: unconditional love, joy, peace, patience, kindheartedness, goodness, faithfulness, gentleness, and self-control.

GALATIANS 5:22–23 VOICE

When you become a follower of Jesus by believing He is the one and only Son of God who died on the cross to remove the penalty of sin once and for all, the Holy Spirit takes up residence in your heart. It is He who enables the *fruit* to grow within and become part of your life in powerful ways. The Spirit is the one who helps transform you from the inside out to live more godly lives. He emboldens you to be different.

Every time you choose to love God with your words and actions, it's because of the Spirit. When you choose to love others with patience, kindness, and gentleness, it's His influence. And when you choose to love yourself enough to embrace joy, peace, and self-control, it's because the Spirit encourages it. Today, thank Him for it all.

LORD, THANK YOU FOR THE GIFT OF THE HOLY SPIRIT! HELP ME RECOGNIZE HIS WORK IN MY LIFE AND FOLLOW IT BOLDLY. AMEN.

It's All about Community

Now since we have chosen to walk with the Spirit,
let's keep each step in perfect sync with God's Spirit.
This will happen when we set aside our self-interests
and work together to create true community instead of
a culture consumed by provocation, pride, and envy.

GALATIANS 5:25–26 VOICE

God is all about community. He created us to thrive in it, even knowing the stress it may bring. Our friends will betray us. Our family will infuriate us. Our teammates will annoy us. Our coworkers will provoke us. And our teachers, coaches, small group leaders, and neighbors will get on our nerves without fail. But community is still a gift when we do it right.

The best thing we can do is choose to love no matter what. We do this by focusing on the needs of others rather than seeking our own interests. Every time we choose to set aside pride and envy, we are encouraging relationships to grow deeper. And when we ask God to help us be kind and full of compassion, He will bless us with true community.

LORD, HELP ME BE A GOOD FRIEND IN EVERY WAY. AMEN.

Why Things Go Sideways

For the whole law comes down to this one instruction: "Love your neighbor as yourself," so why all this vicious gnawing on each other? If you are not careful, you will find you've eaten each other alive!

GALATIANS 5:14–15 VOICE

When love isn't at the core of our relationships, things go sideways. Maybe you've experienced this with a friend who was always jealous of you. Maybe it was someone who treated you like an inconvenience. Maybe someone accused you without any good reason. Or maybe you've been rejected by others because of your faith. There is a strong reason God has called us to love those around us.

Friend, are you following His law of love in your own life? Are you choosing to operate with a heart of compassion? Are you extending kindness to family and friends, even when it's challenging? Ask God for help and let Him tender your nature to love well.

LORD, SOMETIMES I STRUGGLE TO CHOOSE LOVE BECAUSE PEOPLE DRIVE ME NUTS. STRENGTHEN ME SO I CAN TREAT THEM IN WAYS THAT BLESS THEM AND GLORIFY YOU. AMEN.

The Driving Force

If I speak God's Word with power, revealing all his mysteries and making everything plain as day, and if I have faith that says to a mountain, "Jump," and it jumps, but I don't love, I'm nothing.

1 Corinthians 13:2 MSG

It doesn't matter how wonderful you are to others if love isn't your driving force. You may volunteer long hours or work in the church's nursery or support a child in another part of the world, but if it's not motivated by love, God knows. You may be a regular at small group, help your teachers clean their classroom, or work overtime for your boss. But if love isn't the reason, it's lacking in God's eyes.

The Lord wants love to inspire your kindness. He wants your compassion and concern for others to come from deep within your heart. Love matters greatly to God! And when you ask for His help to let it spur you on to share His goodness, He will.

LORD, FILL MY HEART WITH LOVE. AND LET IT MOTIVATE ME TO BLESS OTHERS. LET IT BE MY REASON FOR EMPATHY TOWARD THOSE AROUND ME. AMEN.

He Loved Us So Much

But God is so rich in mercy; he loved us so much that even though we were spiritually dead and doomed by our sins, he gave us back our lives again when he raised Christ from the dead—only by his undeserved favor have we ever been saved.

EPHESIANS 2:4–5 TLB

If there was ever an example of what it looks like to choose love, today's passage of scripture unpacks it perfectly. We weren't cleaned up from our sin. We weren't living godly lives. And we weren't even repentant. Yet God loved us so much that He sent Jesus to bridge the gap our shortcomings created. Jesus stepped off the throne and out of heaven, lived and died and rose again, because we were so loved. The thought of being separated was too much for God, so He made a way.

Today, meditate on this beautiful truth and thank the Lord for His goodness. Share your thoughts, telling Him what this sacrifice says to you. And then let love flow from your full heart, blessing others in meaningful ways.

LORD, THANK YOU FOR YOUR ENDLESS MERCY AND GOODNESS. AMEN.

The Power of God's Love

Your kingdom will never end; Your rule will endure forever. [You are faithful to Your promise, and Your acts are marked with grace.] The Eternal sustains all who stumble on their way. For those who are broken down, God is near. He raises them up in hope.

PSALM 145:13–14 VOICE

No matter what you're going through today, know that God's love is covering you. He is with you always. And because of that, you will have the strength to endure what life has brought your way. His love is a powerful weapon for those who follow Him. God is trustworthy and faithful, which means you're in capable hands. Yes, He is near to you right now.

It's because God chose to first love you that you're now able to extend it to others. Your kindness and compassion can help those around you find strength to stand strong in their own storms. You can be near to them, supporting in meaningful ways. And by choosing to love, you can help bring hope too.

LORD, THANK YOU FOR FIRST LOVING ME SO I CAN CHOOSE TO LOVE YOU AND OTHERS. AMEN.

Blessed by Humility

If you will humble yourselves under the mighty hand of God, in his good time he will lift you up.

1 PETER 5:6 TLB

The Lord loves a humble heart. It's clear throughout scripture that He values the meek. He honors those who are willing to surrender their ways to His. It's not always easy to do, but it's a beautiful act of obedience to the Father, and blessings flow from it. It's choosing to love God more than anything or anyone else.

Where do you need to take a knee to the Lord? In what area of your life are you struggling in your own strength? Where are you being too wise in your own eyes? When you choose to show love to God through letting Him lead, you will find it changes things according to His will and in His perfect timing. And giving up control brings freedom, especially since He is trustworthy in every way.

LORD, HELP ME SEE THE BIGGER PICTURE OF HUMILITY SO I CAN FIND NO REASON NOT TO SURRENDER TO YOU IN LOVE. AMEN.

Your Worries and Cares

Let him have all your worries and cares,
for he is always thinking about you and
watching everything that concerns you.

1 PETER 5:7 TLB

Trusting God enough to give Him the things that worry us is hard. Too often, we cling to them, trying in earnest to fix each situation because we feel we simply can't trust anyone else to do so. And rather than let God bring healing and hope, we hold on for dear life.

When the Lord chose to love you, it encompassed every part of your life. From struggles with friends to battles at home to stressors at school, He wants to help you navigate it all. Whether it's fear of finals or harsh criticism on the court, God wants to unburden you. Whether it's self-doubt or an unwillingness to forgive, He is watching over everything that concerns you. Today, let His love engulf you. And be willing to let God take every worry and care so you can live unstuck.

LORD, THANK YOU FOR CHOOSING TO LOVE ME ENOUGH TO WANT TO CARRY MY BURDENS. WHAT A GIFT. AMEN.

It's Personal

After you have suffered a little while, our God, who is full of kindness through Christ, will give you his eternal glory. He personally will come and pick you up, and set you firmly in place, and make you stronger than ever.

1 PETER 5:10 TLB

You will always be able to love others well because God will always be at work in your life, healing and restoring. Scripture says He will *personally* pick you up when you're down. He will *personally* set you upright. And God promises to *personally* strengthen you again. . .and then some. For Him, it's personal.

Since God won't allow you to suffer and struggle forever, you'll have the ability to be a force of goodness for others. Your hope will return. You will regain your joy and peace and perspective, allowing your heart to be tendered toward family and friends again. God will personally make sure of it.

LORD, IT'S ENCOURAGING TO REALIZE TOUGH SEASONS WILL PASS AND I WILL HAVE THE ENERGY AND DESIRE TO REACH BACK OUT AND LOVE THOSE AROUND ME WITH PASSION. THANK YOU! AMEN.

The Handshake

Give each other the handshake of Christian love. Peace be to all of you who are in Christ.

1 PETER 5:14 TLB

What are some ways you can give others a *handshake of Christian love*? Maybe it's cleaning the kitchen for your mom without her asking. Maybe it's offering to babysit your siblings for the night (and for free) while your parents have a date. Maybe it's making a priority to visit your aging grandparents. It could be helping a neighbor mow the lawn or shovel fresh snow from the walkway. Is there a teacher who could use your help after school? Would it bless your coach to stay late and clean up? Is there a new girl at school who needs a friend?

Ask God to open your eyes and your heart to see needs around you. Then be ready to offer help when needed. Seize opportunities to let others know they are important and loved. And choose to give compassion and kindness whenever God highlights a person or a situation. Choose to love!

LORD, I WANT TO LOVE OTHERS THROUGH MY WORDS AND ACTIONS. PLEASE GUIDE ME! AMEN.

Purposeful Ways to Love

But you are merciful and gentle, Lord, slow in getting angry, full of constant loving-kindness and of truth; so look down in pity and grant strength to your servant and save me.

Psalm 86:15–16 TLB

If you want to be known as someone who loves others well, then watch how God does it and follow His lead. The way He loves is perfect! And while we can't love others unflawed, we can be purposeful. We can put our best foot forward and lead with pure motives. We can be gentle with our words and merciful with our actions. We can stay calm, even when it's not easy. With God's help, we can be ready and willing to lend a hand to those who need it. We can choose to love with hearts full of compassion.

The world is hard enough. Amen? Sometimes the best thing we can do is be a light in the dark. Every time we show compassion rather than criticism or grace over grappling, it makes a huge difference. Listen for God's voice and let Him lead you into purposeful ways to show love to those around you.

LORD, I'M LISTENING! AMEN.

When God Is Added to the Mix

For though we have never yet seen God,
when we love each other God lives in us,
and his love within us grows ever stronger.

1 JOHN 4:12 TLB

When you add God into the mix, you will be able to love like a superhero. How does it work? Today's scripture gives us the supernatural formula.

In our humanity, our hearts are naturally drawn to love certain people. We have our family and friends who receive all our tender hearts have to give. There may be some teachers and coaches who fit into that category too. And we may feel compassion for others along the way. Because God lives in us, we can love one another. It's His presence that also allows that love to grow stronger. It supercharges us to love deeper. And it empowers us to choose to love when others might just walk away.

LORD, YOU ALWAYS MAKE EVERYTHING BETTER. IT'S BECAUSE OF YOUR GENEROUS AND UNCHANGING LOVE THAT I'M ABLE TO CHOOSE TO LOVE OTHERS HERE AND NOW. WHAT A GIFT! AMEN.

Love through Obedience

"The person who has My commandments and keeps them is the one who [really] loves Me; and whoever [really] loves Me will be loved by My Father, and I will love him and reveal Myself to him [I will make Myself real to him]."

JOHN 14:21 AMP

When you choose to love God, that decision automatically means you are also choosing to love His commandments by keeping them. Some people profess their love for the Lord, but their lives tell a different story. They talk about the importance of following His will and ways, but their words are cheap because their actions don't align. And while God isn't expecting perfection from us, He is looking for pure hearts with honest motives.

Ask God to help you follow through on your declared love by being aware of how you talk and how you live. It's important to spend time in the Word because it's where we hear from the Lord and learn what our faith should look like. And it helps us choose to love God with all our heart and mind.

LORD, HELP ME SHOW YOUR LOVE THROUGH HOW I LIVE MY LIFE. AMEN.

Our Flooded Heart

And hope will never fail to satisfy our deepest need because the Holy Spirit that was given to us has flooded our hearts with God's love.

Romans 5:5 voice

Imagine that! As a believer in Jesus Christ, the Holy Spirit living within you floods your heart with God's love. It's not a minimal amount of love. It's not a drop or two. It's not even a good amount. Scripture tells us His love floods our hearts. We are overwhelmed by its abundance, meaning we have a deep well to pull from to love those around us. So, in those moments when we don't want to choose to love the bully, the betrayer, or the brutal, we can find bravery because of His love in us. With God's help, we can decide to extend grace to those who don't deserve it from us. And we can offer compassion with a pure heart, knowing the Holy Spirit will replenish as needed.

LORD, WHAT A GIFT TO KNOW THAT MY FAITH HAS PROMPTED THE HOLY SPIRIT TO FLOOD MY HEART WITH YOUR PERFECT LOVE. HELP ME PULL FROM THAT WELL WHEN I NEED IT THE MOST. AMEN.

Thanking God for Loving Us

My lips praise you because your faithful love is better than life itself!

PSALM 63:3 CEB

Have you told God how grateful you are to have been chosen by Him to love? Today's verse offers a great reminder of the importance of praising the Lord for His goodness. Too often, we take for granted the kindness and compassion He shows us. We see it, but we don't always take the time to tell Him. Friend, let's decide to be women who have thankful hearts and choose to share them with God regularly.

Think about how great it makes you feel when a teammate compliments your efforts in the game. Or when a teacher recognizes your attempts to make a new student feel welcomed. Or when your parents notice that you're honoring their requests without being reminded. Just like we appreciate being seen, God does too. Let's choose to love Him with our grateful hearts every day!

LORD, THANK YOU FOR YOUR FAITHFUL LOVE THAT FOLLOWS ME EVERYWHERE I GO! MY HEART IS FULL OF GRATITUDE FOR THE WAYS YOU BLESS ME! AMEN.

The Choice Is Yours

"You can't worship two gods at once.
Loving one god, you'll end up hating the other.
Adoration of one feeds contempt for the other.
You can't worship God and Money both."
MATTHEW 6:24 MSG

The Bible reminds us that we have a decision to make, and it's not necessarily a one-and-done decision either. Often it's a daily thing that we'll have to decide who we're going to choose to love. Will we pick God to adore, or will we be swayed by what the world promises to provide?

It's so easy to get caught up in the newest trends in clothing, making us jealous to where we crave it for ourselves. We want a new car that rivals our friend's. We want the financial freedom to keep up with those around us. And when these become our focus, it reveals our choice to love money more than God. Be mindful that His heart is for ours to be with Him alone.

LORD, I DON'T WANT TO WORSHIP MONEY OVER YOU. HELP ME KEEP A HEALTHY PERSPECTIVE SO I'M NOT SWAYED IN THE WRONG DIRECTION. I CHOOSE YOU! AMEN.

Others-Focused

Now you can have real love for everyone because your souls have been cleansed from selfishness and hatred when you trusted Christ to save you; so see to it that you really do love each other warmly, with all your hearts.

1 PETER 1:22 TLB

If we surrender our selfish desires to the Lord, He will cleanse our hearts so we are able to think of others above ourselves. It won't matter if we get our way or not. We won't have to be recognized on the field or in the classroom to feel valued. We won't fight to have our opinions heard. And we will have a servant's heart, one that is more concerned about others being cared for instead of always looking out for number one.

Talk to God about your desire to have real love for your friends and family. Tell Him how you want to love strangers through compassion and generosity. Ask Him to fill you with kindness so you're able to bless those you meet. Once you become a believer in Jesus Christ, He promises to replace selfishness with selflessness.

LORD, HELP ME TO REALLY LOVE OTHERS WARMLY AND WITH ALL MY HEART. AMEN.

A Secured Eternity

Anyone who loves Me will listen to My voice and obey. The Father will love him, and We will draw close to him and make a dwelling place within him. The one who does not love Me ignores My message, which is not from Me, but from the Father who sent Me.

JOHN 14:23–24 VOICE

Simply put, when you accept Jesus as your personal Savior, God will come close, and His Spirit will dwell within you. And it's because of that acceptance you will want to love God by listening and obeying His commands found in the Bible. Your choice to follow Him will help you choose to grow in your relationship daily.

But, friend, if you are choosing to ignore the Lord and disobey His will and ways, let that be a red flag. Talk to God about it. Talk to a trusted Christ follower who can share wisdom and guidance. And make sure your salvation in eternity is secured.

LORD, I WANT TO KNOW YOU MORE AND GROW IN MY LOVE FOR YOU. HELP ME CHOOSE YOU DAILY. AMEN.

Love One Another

*So, my loved ones, if God loved us so sacrificially,
surely we should love one another.*

1 JOHN 4:11 VOICE

We have no acceptable excuse to not choose to love others with gusto. Even if they are mean, even if they annoy us, even if they are selfish, we are called to love. Even if they treat us badly or ignore us altogether, we are called to love. And even if they can't stand us for our faith, our choices, or our values, we are still called to love. That's why we need God's help.

Choosing to love others isn't a call to be mistreated. We don't have to let them abuse or belittle us. They don't get a free pass to put us down at every turn. And sometimes, the best way we can love others is with healthy boundaries in place. What God wants is for our heart to be full of compassion and not loathing. We're to choose it so we aren't the ones initiating or returning unkindness. Because God loves us, we can love those around us, no matter what.

LORD, HELP ME LOVE OTHERS. AMEN.

When Trust Is Hard

Tell me all about your faithful love come morning time, because I trust you. Show me the way I should go, because I offer my life up to you.

Psalm 143:8 CEB

When we love God with all our heart, we find ourselves able to trust again. Maybe trust is hard for you because someone broke it and left a big wound. Maybe you've been betrayed more than you care to share. Or maybe someone lied and broke your heart, making it hard to place your faith in someone again. Big hugs.

But friend, be encouraged! God's love is unflawed and faithful. His track record is perfect, and His plans for your life are always to benefit you, even if it's hard to see that at times. And when you choose to believe in His goodness and trust in His promises, you will be able to surrender to the Lord with confidence. You will once again be able to trust.

LORD, YOU KNOW THE PAIN OF BETRAYAL I'VE FELT AND THE STRUGGLE TO OPEN MY HEART AGAIN AND TRUST. BUT I CHOOSE TO LOVE YOU AND LET YOU LEAD. AMEN.

Let God Handle It

Make me live again, Lord, for your name's sake. Bring me out of distress because of your righteousness. Wipe out my enemies because of your faithful love. Destroy everyone who attacks me, because I am your servant.

Psalm 143:11–12 CEB

When you find yourself in a difficult situation with others, let God be the one who saves you. So often, we think it's up to us. We decide we have to handle things on our own. And rather than choose to love our enemies, we make it our mission to fight back and get even. But scripture reminds us that our Father is willing and able to make things right for us.

Friend, every time you feel the need to battle, go right to God in prayer. In those moments when you feel the need to confront others in anger, ask Him to respond on your behalf. The Lord wants us to choose to love our enemies and pray for them. Let God handle everything else.

LORD, HELP ME TRUST THAT YOU WILL HANDLE MY ENEMIES SO I AM FREE TO LOVE AS YOU COMMAND. AMEN.

Instead, Love

Do not seek revenge or hold a grudge against any of your people. Instead, love your neighbor as you love yourself, for I am the Eternal One.

Leviticus 19:18 VOICE

When a friend turns on you, or a coach plays favorites against you, or a sibling ignores requests to stay out of your room and breaks something of great value, how can you choose to love rather than sit in anger or hurt? The truth is that it'll take God's help. No doubt about it. On our own, we'd naturally lean toward holding a grudge or entertaining vengeful thoughts. But the Lord is clear about His desire in these kinds of circumstances.

At every opportunity—easy or hard—be mindful to keep your heart pure. And when you start to lose your cool, ask God to help you choose love over everything else. It may be the toughest thing you have to walk out, but He will bless you each time you do.

LORD, HELP ME FOLLOW YOUR PLAN FOR CHOOSING LOVE INSTEAD OF HATE. BECAUSE I SIMPLY CANNOT DO IT WITHOUT YOU. AMEN.

Loving Your Enemies

"There is a saying, 'Love your friends and hate your enemies.' But I say: Love your enemies! Pray for those who persecute you!"

MATTHEW 5:43–44 TLB

This is one of those hard-to-imagine passages of scripture. It may even feel impossible to walk out. But the reality is that the Lord wants us to not only pray for our enemies but also love them. He wants us to respond with compassion even when they're snarky toward us. Too often, we match their emotions without even realizing it. When they get angry, we get angry back. We withhold forgiveness because they are withholding it too. And we give the same silent treatment they're dishing us. Friend, this isn't what God wants. This isn't choosing love.

Ask the Lord for the ability to follow this command. He understands the struggle to love those who mistreat you. The challenge doesn't catch Him off guard. And when you pray in earnest for the heart to show kindness at all times, He will equip you to do so.

LORD, I CAN'T CHOOSE TO LOVE MY ENEMIES UNLESS YOU HELP ME. PLEASE DO! AMEN.

The Gift of Freedom

Brothers and sisters, God has called you to freedom! Hear the call, and do not spoil this gift by using your liberty to engage in what your flesh desires; instead, use it to serve each other as Jesus taught through love.

GALATIANS 5:13 VOICE

Today's scripture reminds us to be careful with the gift of freedom. We're to handle it with care, honoring God in the ways we use it. This kind of intentionality is pleasing because it shows how much we care. It's choosing to love the Lord through obedience. And it's setting aside our fleshly desires—those things we want that don't glorify God—and instead using self-control in our choices.

Let's decide we want to be big-hearted in the ways we honor the Lord and serve others with our time and treasure. Let's love our friends and family in meaningful ways that reflect how we truly feel about them. And let's use our freedom responsibly so we're a blessing to those around us.

LORD, GIVE ME THE DESIRE TO USE THE FREEDOM I'VE BEEN GIVEN IN GODLY WAYS. AMEN.

Selfless and Sacrificial Love

So Jacob served Laban for seven years in exchange for Rachel. The years went by quickly and seemed to him to be only a few days because of the immense love he had for her.

GENESIS 29:20 VOICE

Jacob loved Rachel so deeply that he agreed to work for her father for seven years so he could earn her hand in marriage. That's a long time, but to Jacob, it went by quickly. Scripture says it only felt like a few days to him. Now, that is selfless and sacrificial love and a wonderful example God chose to include in His Word. What might He want you to glean from it?

To Jacob, there was nothing he wouldn't do for Rachel. Long hours that turned into long months that turned into long years never deterred him. Laboring at the will of Laban didn't concern him. He chose to love her with his whole self. What speaks to you most about this account? How does it challenge you? What changes need to be made?

LORD, HELP ME LEARN TO LOVE YOU AND OTHERS SELFLESSLY AND SACRIFICIALLY. AMEN.

Making a Clean Break

Make a clean break with all cutting, backbiting, profane talk. Be gentle with one another, sensitive. Forgive one another as quickly and thoroughly as God in Christ forgave you.

EPHESIANS 4:31–32 MSG

If your goal is choosing to love those around you as best as you can, then today's scripture gives you a road map to follow. To some it may seem like common sense, but it's always smart to let God refocus your heart from time to time. The truth is, it's easy to let attitudes and actions slip. And when we do, bad habits begin to form. Sometimes it takes God's Word to wake us up to the ways we've been treating those who we really care about.

Are you regularly backtalking to a parent? Have you been judgmental in your comments toward a sibling? Have you been insensitive to a friend? Are cuss words sneaking into your vocabulary? Are you holding on to anger, punishing the one who hurt you? Talk to God about these things and ask Him to help you follow His road map so you can choose to love others well.

LORD, KEEP ME FOCUSED ON YOUR ROAD MAP SO I BLESS THOSE AROUND ME. AMEN.

The Enemy's Invitation

If you are angry, don't sin by nursing your grudge. Don't let the sun go down with you still angry—get over it quickly; for when you are angry, you give a mighty foothold to the devil.

EPHESIANS 4:26–27 TLB

We all get mad from time to time. It's a normal response to life, especially when facing challenging circumstances and frustrating people. But every time we get angry, it's an invitation for the enemy to gain a foothold in our lives. In most situations, we're able to forgive and move on. There are times, however, when we hold on to that anger way too long.

This is why it's important we choose to love, even when it takes all we've got. Clinging to our irritation—while we may feel it's justified—allows the enemy to mess with us. He fuels the flames of fury within us. And rather than show compassion and kindness, we put up walls or burn down bridges. So be quick to extend grace and release anger. Choose to love instead.

LORD, HELP ME KEEP SHORT ACCOUNTS SO I DON'T LET ANGER RULE MY LIFE. AMEN.

Saying What Is Good and Helpful

Don't use bad language. Say only what is good and helpful to those you are talking to, and what will give them a blessing.

EPHESIANS 4:29 TLB

Consider how great you feel when someone congratulates you on the win. Or when a teacher recognizes your effort in class. Or when a friend's testimony includes sharing about the instrumental part you played in her success. Or when a parent brags to others in front of you about how your persistence paid off. It makes you feel adored and valued, right?

God wants us to be mindful about our words too. We need to think before we speak to make sure what we want to say is full of truth and love. Used the right way, words are powerful tools because they can affirm and encourage in wonderful ways. They can help bring comfort and hope to a weary heart. And when you say only what is good and helpful, it reveals how much you care. Choose to love with your words.

LORD, HELP ME THINK BEFORE I SPEAK. CHOOSING THE RIGHT WORDS TO CONVEY HOW MUCH I CARE. AMEN.

Committing Murder with Thoughts

"You're familiar with the command to the ancients, 'Do not murder.' I'm telling you that anyone who is so much as angry with a brother or sister is guilty of murder. Carelessly call a brother 'idiot!' and you just might find yourself hauled into court. Thoughtlessly yell 'stupid!' at a sister and you are on the brink of hellfire. The simple moral fact is that words kill."

MATTHEW 5:21–22 MSG

It may sound dramatic, but Jesus tells us that when we're angry, we are guilty of murder. Why? Because in our irritation, we're busy wishing the worst on those who have made us mad. Think about it. How often have you wished someone would fail or be exposed or be wiped from the face of the planet? We think of those ideas as innocent and fleeting, but to God they are much more than that. Words—even words uttered in our hearts and minds—have the power to be destructive.

Today, spend time repenting for all the times your thoughts took a wrong turn. For the horrible ways you hoped for someone's failure, confess. Admit the plans for revenge you cooked up. And choose to love others by taking control of any angry thoughts about them.

LORD, HELP MY THOUGHTS BE LOVING. AMEN.

A Servant's Heart

Don't let selfishness and prideful agendas take over. Embrace true humility, and lift your heads to extend love to others. Get beyond yourselves and protecting your own interests; be sincere, and secure your neighbors' interests first.

PHILIPPIANS 2:3–4 VOICE

Having a servant's heart can be hard to do because we're programmed by the world to care about ourselves first. We are taught to look out for number one at all costs. And rather than living focused on the needs of others, we often find ourselves overwhelmed by our own needs. We decide to protect our interests, leaving those around us lacking. This grieves God's heart.

Every day, you get to choose whether to have compassion or not. You decide if you'll be selfless or selfish. It's up to you to be humble or prideful, sincere or fake. But if you want to follow God's command and choose to love, then ask Him to create in you a servant's heart.

LORD, BREAK MY HEART FOR WHAT BREAKS YOURS. HELP ME BE FOCUSED ON OTHERS SO THEY WILL KNOW YOUR GOODNESS. AMEN.

Be a Shining Star

Do all things without complaining or bickering with each other, so you will be found innocent and blameless; you are God's children called to live without a single stain on your reputations among this perverted and crooked generation. Shine like stars across the land.

PHILIPPIANS 2:14–15 VOICE

We are most certainly living in a perverted and crooked generation. There is no doubt about it. And friend, it's only going to get crazier. But you are a child of God, which comes with immeasurable benefits, so take heart and be encouraged! Stay focused on His will and each command, and you'll be okay. And while you won't live a perfect life, you are called to live a purposeful one. You are told to pursue righteousness. Lean on Him as He guides you through each day.

God wants you to be free of complaining and bickering with others. It's not helpful nor does it bring encouragement. He wants you to be unstained by the world. And when you love Him through obedience, you'll stand out. Your faith will shine.

LORD, LET MY FAITH SHINE BRIGHTLY FOR YOU! AMEN.

When Bragging Is Good

There is no one like Timothy. What sets him apart from others is his deep concern for you and your spiritual journey. This is rare, my friends, for most people only care about themselves, not about what is dear to the heart of Jesus the Anointed.

PHILIPPIANS 2:20–21 VOICE

Paul is bragging about Timothy, sharing with others what a wonderful man he is. He is supporting his friend by speaking kindly about him. He is proudly talking about Timothy's goodness and where his heart lies. And by doing so, Paul is opening the door for others to appreciate what Timothy has to offer. What a gift!

You can do the same for those in your life too. Always have good things to say about others, talking them up whenever the chance arises. Be generous and honest in how you speak about people. Show them in the best light possible. And know that by doing so, you're honoring them in loving ways.

LORD, HELP ME BRAG ON THOSE I LOVE. LET ME ALWAYS SPEAK OF THEM WITH KINDNESS AND GENEROSITY. AMEN.

Seeking God Diligently

"I love those who love me; and those who seek me early and diligently will find me."
PROVERBS 8:17 AMP

Do you ever feel like God is far away from you, like your prayers bounce off the ceiling rather than reach the heavens? This is a common feeling for most of us from time to time. And it's unsettling. But the issue isn't God.

The Lord is clear in today's scripture and throughout His Word that when we seek God with care and persistence, we will find Him. It's not that He is hiding. Relationship isn't a game for God. But He is seeking an authentic heart, surrendered and expectant. Are you praying with uncertainty? Are you just going through the motions? Are you attentive as you pray or easily distracted by something else? Just like we can tell when people aren't genuine, God can too. And when we seek Him from shallow places, He knows it. So, choose to love the Lord deeply, focusing only on Him as you pray. Seek God diligently.

LORD, I WANT TO GIVE YOU MY FULL ATTENTION. SHOW ME HOW TO SEEK YOU WITH PASSION AND PURPOSE. AMEN.

The Controlling Force

You see, the controlling force in our lives is the love of the Anointed One. And our confession is this: One died for all; therefore, all have died.

2 CORINTHIANS 5:14 VOICE

When God's love is the controlling force in your life, it will allow you to treat strangers with compassion rather than contempt. It will help you show respect to your teachers no matter how they treat you. You'll be able to respect your coaches and bosses, even when their treatment feels unfair. When God's love drives you, you'll find ways to engage regularly with your annoying siblings. You will take your parents' rules to heart and walk them out with gratitude. You'll understand the sacrifice of Jesus and appreciate the need for community. And you will love the Lord and His commands, pursuing righteous living every day.

At every opportunity, choose to love others with His love. Let it be what leads you. Let it be the center of each friendship and relationship with family. Let God's love be your controlling force.

LORD, I CAN LOVE WITH PURPOSE BECAUSE YOU FIRST LOVED ME. AMEN.

Overwhelming and Wonderful

I love you, God—you make me strong.
God is bedrock under my feet, the castle
in which I live, my rescuing knight.

Psalm 18:1 MSG

Knowing how much God loves us is overwhelming and wonderful at the same time. No matter how wretched we are to Him, or to our friends, or to our family, His love never waivers. When we cheat on a test, lie to a parent, steal from work, or gossip behind a friend's back, God's love is steadfast. When we struggle with unbelief or are tangled in a season of sinning, the Lord's heart for us is still good. Just wow!

There is nothing you can do to make Him love you any more or any less than He does at this very moment. Thankfully, God's compassion doesn't hinge on our performance. But friend, let's live faithfully as best as we can so He knows our love for Him too. Let's choose God over anything the world has to offer.

LORD, YOU ARE THE BEDROCK UNDER MY FEET. THE CASTLE WHERE I LIVE. AND MY STRENGTH. THANK YOU FOR LOVING ME! AMEN.

Always and Forever the Savior

He reached down from heaven and took me and drew me out of my great trials. He rescued me from deep waters. He delivered me from my strong enemy, from those who hated me—I who was helpless in their hands.

PSALM 18:16–17 TLB

When you find yourself in tough circumstances, God will be the one to rescue and deliver. You'll have friends to offer a listening ear, give you a caring hug, and love you through the hard times. Family will stand strong in support, walking with you through the messy moments. A small group leader or counselor may help you navigate the ups and downs you'll face. But it will be God who reaches down from heaven and pulls you out of the deep water threatening to pull you under.

The Lord puts wonderful people in your life who will choose to love you through the good and bad. You will do the same for them. God, however, will always and forever be who saves. Hold that truth tightly.

LORD, THANK YOU FOR RESCUING AND DELIVERING ME. ALWAYS. AMEN.

Doing What Is Right

And so the Lord has paid me with his blessings,
for I have done what is right, and I am pure of heart.
This he knows, for he watches my every step.
Psalm 18:24 TLB

Every time you choose to love others, you're doing what is right in God's eyes. When you invite the new girl into your group of friends, or offer free babysitting to the single mom, or volunteer your time to do yardwork for an elderly neighbor, it's an act of love. And when your motives are genuine and authentic, God clearly sees your heart and is pleased.

Be the kind of young woman who wants to do what is right, knowing it matters to the Lord. Not only will it yield blessings for you, but it will also show God you're choosing to love Him through compassionate acts toward others. Friend, let faith guide you into righteous living each day!

LORD, KEEP MY HEART WHOLESOME AND UNTAINTED SO I'M ABLE TO FAITHFULLY LIVE OUT EACH DAY DOING WHAT IS RIGHT IN YOUR EYES. AMEN.

Cared For Daily

He fills me with strength and protects me wherever I go. He gives me the surefootedness of a mountain goat upon the crags. He leads me safely along the top of the cliffs. He prepares me for battle and gives me strength to draw an iron bow!

PSALM 18:32–34 TLB

What a wonderful and faithful God we serve! There is nothing we will face that He won't prepare us for. There won't be any situations too difficult for us. No painful circumstances we won't be able to weather. At every turn, God will provide us with strength and wisdom and stamina. He will allow us to stand strong and face suffering with courage. He'll lead us through the tricky terrain of trials with precision. And we will find every kind of support as we take the next right step in faith.

This is why you can confidently choose to love God with all your heart. Without fail, you can fully trust you are loved and seen and will be cared for daily.

LORD, YOU ARE A GOOD, GOOD FATHER! MY HEART IS WITH YOU BECAUSE I KNOW YOUR HEART IS ALWAYS WITH ME. AMEN.

Unselfish Concern for Others

If, however, you are [really] fulfilling the royal law according to the Scripture, "You shall love your neighbor as yourself [that is, if you have an unselfish concern for others and do things for their benefit]" you are doing well.

James 2:8 AMP

What does unselfish concern for others look like? Maybe you offer to deep clean the house for your mom, no strings attached. Maybe you sponsor a child from across the world, committing to financially support them monthly. Maybe you invest time doing things with siblings, pouring into them weekly. Maybe you shovel snow or mow lawns for neighbors who can't easily handle the tasks. Or maybe you tutor students because you want to see them succeed. What other ideas can you come up with?

The key is choosing to love those around you by meeting their needs without keeping score. Let there be no expectation of a payback. Just decide to show kindness and compassion because God has asked it of you.

LORD, HELP ME LOVE OTHERS WITH UNSELFISH CONCERN AND ALWAYS FOR THEIR BENEFIT RATHER THAN MINE. AMEN.

Deep Roots

And I pray that Christ will be more and more at home in your hearts, living within you as you trust in him. May your roots go down deep into the soil of God's marvelous love.

EPHESIANS 3:17 TLB

The more time you spend in God's presence, the deeper your roots of faith grow. Investing in your relationship with Him helps you better understand how much He loves you. It helps you embrace that you're chosen and valued. It settles your spirit and brings a sense of belonging. And it allows you to trust God better because you've seen His goodness produced in your life.

There are beautiful benefits that come from choosing to love the Lord and letting Him sow a deeper faith into your life. Not only does it strengthen your resolve and intertwine your heart to His, but it gives you compassion as you love those around you. As you grow closer to God, you'll blossom and bloom as a believer in unexpected and wonderful ways.

LORD, HELP THE ROOTS OF MY FAITH GO DOWN DEEP IN THE SOUL OF YOUR MARVELOUS LOVE! AMEN.

Infinite Love

With all of Your people they will have the power to understand that the love of the Anointed is infinitely long, wide, high, and deep, surpassing everything anyone previously experienced. God, may Your fullness flood through their entire beings.

Ephesians 3:18–19 VOICE

It's hard to understand it when scripture says God's love is *infinite*. The dictionary defines it as limitless or endless. It means it's impossible to evaluate or calculate. There is no beginning or end. It's unbroken in length, width, height, and depth. There is nothing to measure it against. And no matter what we do to mess up, we'll never see the end of it. How wonderful!

God chooses to love us eternally, offering a powerful example of how we can choose to love others. Not that we can match His awesomeness (or even come close), but we can ask the Lord to help us love in wonderful ways. We can ask Him to profoundly tender our hearts. And we can choose to extend grace and keep short accounts of wrongs.

LORD, LET YOUR LOVE BE MY EXAMPLE OF HOW TO LOVE OTHERS. AMEN.

Love Like Jesus

Be full of love for others, following the example of Christ who loved you and gave himself to God as a sacrifice to take away your sins. And God was pleased, for Christ's love for you was like sweet perfume to him.

EPHESIANS 5:2 TLB

God is asking us to follow Jesus' example of love. What makes it so special? First and foremost, it is sacrificial. Christ willingly gave up His life so we could have it to the fullest. His compassion was driven by the thought of our future. In His great love, Jesus wanted us to be with Him in heaven forever. And to God, the aroma of His love was sweet.

If we model ourselves after Christ, it means we love sacrificially too. We put the needs of others before ours. We're willing to set aside our plans and ideas to meet the needs of others, all motivated by a generous spirit. And we care about their future, doing what we can today to usher in goodness tomorrow.

LORD, THANK YOU FOR SHOWING ME HOW TO LOVE. EMPOWER ME TO FOLLOW YOUR EXAMPLE SO I CAN LOVE LIKE JESUS. AMEN.

Clean, Wholesome, Pure

Dirty stories, foul talk, and coarse jokes—
these are not for you. Instead, remind each
other of God's goodness, and be thankful.

EPHESIANS 5:4 TLB

Our focus should be steadied by God's goodness. It should be what starts our day and brings it to a close. In tough times, reminding one another about the ways He has shown up is what will bring us comfort. Peace will flood our hearts as we share stories about God's generosity and kindness. And in it all, being mindful to keep our stories clean, our talk wholesome, and our jokes pure will honor the Lord.

There's enough impurity in the world these days. You'll find no shortage of the dirty, foul, and filthy. But you can set a new standard with your friends and family. You can set the example for others to follow. And you can choose to love God with your words and love others by steering them toward His commands.

LORD, HELP ME SHOW OTHERS THE IMPORTANCE OF MY FAITH THROUGH HOW I SPEAK. LET MY WORDS ALWAYS BE HONORING. AMEN.

Powerfully Impacting for the Kingdom

So be careful how you act; these are difficult days. Don't be fools; be wise: make the most of every opportunity you have for doing good. Don't act thoughtlessly, but try to find out and do whatever the Lord wants you to.

EPHESIANS 5:15–17 TLB

What a wonderful commission on how to live a life of faith in a crazy world. Let the wisdom shared in these verses be an encouragement to live every day and navigate every relationship with great intention. God wants you to take every word to heart, doing your best to be present for those you care about—your friends, family, teammates, coworkers, or small group members. These people give you the perfect opportunity to follow the Lord's leading and love them well.

So be wise with your words and actions. Look for ways to bless those around you. Ask the Lord to open your eyes to see where you can do good for the kingdom. And ask God to guide each step of your day so you can powerfully impact your community in beautiful ways.

LORD, SHOW ME HOW TO CHOOSE LOVE WITH PASSION AND PURPOSE. AMEN.

Giving Thanks Always

Talk with each other much about the Lord, quoting psalms and hymns and singing sacred songs, making music in your hearts to the Lord. Always give thanks for everything to our God and Father in the name of our Lord Jesus Christ.

EPHESIANS 5:19–20 TLB

Consider that when we're told to *always give thanks for everything*, it's an intentional decision to love the Lord with a grateful heart. Even when we face challenging circumstances and stinky situations, there is always something to thank God for. Even when we're full of fear and unsteady with worry, we can find a reason to be appreciative.

Love the Lord with your thanksgiving! As a matter of fact, let it be a weapon to battle the enemy. When you're angry at a parent, or frustrated with a boss, or hurt by a friend, go to God in prayer and tell Him all the reasons you are grateful for Him. Praise is a mighty tool in the hands of a believer.

LORD, THANK YOU FOR BEING OVER ALL THINGS EARTHLY OR HEAVENLY. I PRAISE YOUR MAGNIFICENCE! AMEN.

The Blessing of Friendship

Friends come and friends go, but a true friend sticks by you like family.

PROVERBS 18:24 MSG

Not all friends are lifers. To understand that early in life is a gift! There are some who are seasonal friends, there for a time and then gone. There are other relationships that last longer and are deeper, but they eventually come to an end as well. And then there are the sweetest of friendships that span years and years. These are the ones who walk through the ups and downs of life. Because you have such history together, they feel more like family.

Friendship is a wonderful blessing to cherish and hold dear, but not all are lifers, and that is okay! Regardless, choose to love each friend with purpose. Enjoy the time God has given you together. And be the kind of friend you want them to be to you.

LORD, I'M GRATEFUL FOR THE FRIENDSHIPS YOU'VE BLESSED ME WITH. EVEN IN THE HARD TIMES. AND EVEN WHEN THEY DON'T LAST. THANK YOU FOR SURROUNDING ME WITH PEOPLE TO DO LIFE WITH. HELP ME LOVE THEM WELL! AMEN.

The Sharpening of Friends

In the same way that iron sharpens iron,
a person sharpens the character of his friend.

PROVERBS 27:17 VOICE

Part of loving a friend well is being willing to have the hard conversations. It means you call them out for making bad choices. You point out the places where they're not following God's will. You challenge the rude way they're treating others. It means you care for their future enough to keep them on the straight and narrow. And when there is trouble between the two of you, there's an honest discussion to hash it out.

Being the kind of friend who won't walk away when things get hard isn't for the faint of heart. It takes grit to stay connected. It requires a deep care and appreciation for one another. And when you choose to love no matter what, it helps you grow individually and deepen your friendship. How beautiful.

LORD, GIVE ME STRENGTH TO NOT WALK AWAY FROM A FRIENDSHIP WHEN IT GETS HARD. HELP ME TRUST YOU ARE WORKING IN IT AND THROUGH IT TO SMOOTH ROUGH EDGES. AMEN.

Committing to Community

Two can accomplish more than twice as much as one, for the results can be much better. If one falls, the other pulls him up; but if a man falls when he is alone, he's in trouble.

ECCLESIASTES 4:9–10 TLB

We need others in our life to help us walk it out well. We need friends to support us through the heartbreaks that rock our world. We need them to stand with us as we take the next right step, especially when it's difficult or intimidating. We need family to surround us when we feel destabilized by hard moments. We need others who will advocate on our behalf when we're feeling lost or weak. God never intended for us to navigate life alone.

Ask the Lord to bless you with a strong group of friends and family to build you up when you need it the most. And be that pillar of love and steadfastness for them too. Commit to community every day and in every way. Then watch as God blesses it!

LORD, FILL MY HEART WITH LOVE AND MY LIFE WITH GOOD PEOPLE! AMEN.

No Solo Living

Also, if two lie down together, they can stay warm. But how can anyone stay warm alone? Also, one can be overpowered, but two together can put up resistance. A three-ply cord doesn't easily snap.

ECCLESIASTES 4:11–12 CEB

There are times and seasons when we choose to hunker down and go it alone. Maybe it's because of a hard semester schedule. Maybe it's because we feel unloved or unseen by those around us. It could be because we're an introvert and alone time is necessary to regroup mentally and emotionally. Maybe we're nursing a whopper of a broken heart. Or maybe it's because it feels safer to hide away. But be careful.

Scripture reminds us that being alone isn't God's hope for believers. It may be okay for a season but not for long. There are blessings that come from togetherness—blessings that don't accompany solo living. Choosing to love one another is a gift that keeps on giving.

LORD, DON'T LET ME HIDE AWAY FROM COMMUNITY, EVEN WHEN IT'S HARD. INSTEAD, HELP ME EMBRACE FRIENDSHIPS WITH EXCITEMENT AND AN OPEN HEART. AMEN.

Bad Company Corrupts

But don't be so naïve—there's another saying you know well—Bad company corrupts good habits.

1 CORINTHIANS 15:33 VOICE

Today's scripture is a strong reminder to be smart about relationships. The truth is that we are who we hang out with. If you spend time with those engaging in the wrong things—like drugs, alcohol, and inappropriate intimacy—corruption will happen. Thinking you're strong enough to withstand the pressure is naive. God wants something different for you.

Love yourself enough to find godly friends. They won't be perfect, but they will be seeking the Lord in how they live their life. Just as bad company corrupts, good company blesses. Ask God to bring you the right friends who can influence you to pursue righteous living. And then choose to love one another through the hills and valleys life brings.

LORD, NOT ONLY DO I WANT TO FIND THE RIGHT FRIENDS FOR ME. BUT I ALSO WANT TO BE THE RIGHT FRIEND TO THEM. GUIDE ME INTO MUTUALLY BENEFICIAL FRIENDSHIPS WHERE YOU ARE GLORIFIED. AMEN.

A Source of Encouragement

He died for us so that we can live with him forever, whether we are dead or alive at the time of his return. So encourage each other to build each other up, just as you are already doing.

1 THESSALONIANS 5:10–11 TLB

We can show our love for others by being a consistent source of encouragement. They need to be reminded God is still in the business of miracles. They need to know the Lord hears their prayers, and He promises to save. People need to be pointed to the one who brings comfort and restores peace to the weary. And friend, you can do that for those you love.

In this crazy world, God is our anchor. He's why we can stand strong when life gets hard. He is how we stay hopeful when a situation looks discouraging. God is the reason we can be joyful regardless of what's happening around us. And every time we encourage another believer to press into the Lord, it's because we're choosing to love.

LORD, LET ME BE A SOURCE OF REASSURANCE AND INSPIRATION TO THE DOWNTRODDEN. LET ME ALWAYS BE QUICK TO POINT THE DISCOURAGED TO YOU. AMEN.

A Road Map to Loving Others

Dear brothers, warn those who are lazy, comfort those who are frightened, take tender care of those who are weak, and be patient with everyone. See that no one pays back evil for evil, but always try to do good to each other and to everyone else.

1 THESSALONIANS 5:14–15 TLB

Today's verse provides a significant road map to showing love toward others. With complete clarity, Paul gives details on weighty ways to bless those around us. And each time we choose to walk this out, it's an act of love for them and an act of obedience to God.

When your friend is worried about their grades or making the team, remind them to trust God. When someone is feeling weak and close to making a bad decision, sound the alarm. For those lazy in their faith and in their life, challenge them to move forward in positive ways. Be patient with friends who are navigating a tough season of sin. Treat your family with care and compassion. There is no better way to show love.

LORD, I WANT TO BE INTENTIONAL IN MY RELATIONSHIPS WITH OTHERS. GUIDE ME. AMEN.

Sweetness of Counsel

Oil and perfume make the heart glad;
so does the sweetness of a friend's
counsel that comes from the heart.
PROVERBS 27:9 AMP

Consider that when a friend takes the time to talk through a tough situation with you, listening to your challenges and struggles, they are showing you deep love. As they ask questions to gain a better understanding of your hurt, it's because they care about your heart. And when they offer you godly wisdom—wisdom that aligns with God's Word—there's a sweetness to it.

What creates the wonderful aroma is knowing their counsel is heartfelt. Hopefully, it comes from their time spent with the Lord and is an overflow of their own faith. Ask God to confirm their advice is rooted in His wisdom and laced with divine discernment. Then trust that the Lord is using them to bring encouragement, offering direction that will not only bless you but also glorify Him.

LORD, I LOVE THE GIFT OF COMMUNITY, ESPECIALLY WHEN YOU USE IT IN STRATEGIC WAYS TO BLESS ME AND GUIDE ME THROUGH THE MESSY TIMES OF LIFE. AMEN.

Hard Conversations with Friends

Faithful are the wounds of a friend [who corrects out of love and concern], but the kisses of an enemy are deceitful [because they serve his hidden agenda].

PROVERBS 27:6 AMP

Ask the Lord to help you love others with pure motives. Let Him help you keep intentions honest so your heart for others is untainted by selfishness. To thrive in fellowship with other believers, it's important to build this kind of trust with one another. That way, when the hard conversations come, there's a strong foundation already in place.

There will be times we show love for someone by calling them out on bad behavior. We may love them enough to hold them accountable, even though it could be unpleasant. And in our deep love, challenging their negative thought patterns may be necessary to help them find hope. When we're consistently kind and compassionate regardless of the ups and downs, those hard conversations will be received in love.

LORD, LET MY LOVE ALWAYS SHINE THROUGH WHEN I'M HONEST WITH MY FRIENDS AND SHARE WORRIES AND CONCERNS. AMEN.

Why Your Kindness Matters

"For the despairing man there should be kindness from his friend; so that he does not abandon (turn away from) the fear of the Almighty."

JOB 6:14 AMP

One of the reasons God commands us to love others is because it helps maintain their faith in God. Consider that when a friend is having a tough time and we turn our back on them, it can plunge them into the pit of despair. They may feel a huge sense of hopelessness. They may feel rejected by us or abandoned by God. And when we walk away in their moment of desperate need, it may be what throws them over the edge.

Be the first to reach out when a friend is struggling. Choose to love them by being available. Let them know they're loved and seen and most worthy of your time. Pray with them and for them. And know that when you do, you're helping them stay anchored to the Lord and trusting Him for hope and healing.

LORD, OPEN MY EYES TO SEE THOSE WHO NEED MY KINDNESS AND FRIENDSHIP. GIVE ME THE WORDS TO BRING THE RIGHT ENCOURAGEMENT AT THE RIGHT TIME. AMEN.

Who Are You Hanging Out With?

Become wise by walking with the wise; hang out with fools and watch your life fall to pieces.

PROVERBS 13:20 MSG

Do you want to be more joy-filled? Then be around joyful people. Do you want to learn to embrace peace in problematic moments? Try spending time in the presence of peacekeepers. If you desire a greater measure of faith, be sure to hang out with those who are faith giants. Want to be wiser? Then surround yourself with people who seek God in their decisions. It matters who you choose to keep company with.

Today's verse is crystal clear, and we should take it to heart. Who we interact with on the regular absolutely impacts how we think and act. When God created the idea of community, He did so knowing the power it would hold. And when we're around the right people, it's the perfect opportunity to influence one another for kingdom work. We can love one another with purpose and passion!

LORD, HELP ME CHOOSE TO INVEST MY TIME AND HEART IN THOSE WHO WILL POINT ME TO YOU. AMEN.

Don't Be a Wrecking Ball

Destructive people produce conflict;
gossips alienate close friends.
PROVERBS 16:28 CEB

One of the best ways we can love others is to be a peaceful friend. Even in conflict, we can choose to communicate with kindness. There's no need to go *scorched earth* when we're offended. We don't need to blow up the bridge when our feelings get hurt. And we should never run to tell others how we've been insulted or slighted. Honestly, it's none of their business and only serves a selfish purpose.

Instead, let's choose to be women who cling to God when there's a struggle in our relationships. Let's talk to Him and share our heart, unpacking all the feels through prayer. Let's ask for strength, wisdom, and discernment to handle each circumstance with a faith response. And let's be sure we don't come in like a wrecking ball, being destructive for the sake of making a point. With God, we can be loving and kind even in the hardest and most hurtful situations.

LORD, HELP ME RESPOND TO EVERY MESSY MOMENT IN WAYS THAT BLESS OTHERS AND GLORIFY YOU. AMEN.

Don't Stop Meeting Together

And let us consider each other carefully for the purpose of sparking love and good deeds. Don't stop meeting together with other believers, which some people have gotten into the habit of doing. Instead, encourage each other, especially as you see the day drawing near.

HEBREWS 10:24–25 CEB

Spending time in community is important and vital. The problem is that many of us have been hurt by the church, and we use our pain to justify walking away. Instead of forgiving and moving on, we stop participating in church altogether.

But friend, God is clear in His command to meet together. Believers need to be with other believers because it sparks brotherly (and sisterly) love. It enables us to do good deeds with passion and purpose. It brings much-needed encouragement to stay faithful until the end. And it's how we love and feel it in return.

LORD, HEAL MY HEART FROM ANY HURT I MAY BE HOLDING ON TO. KEEP ME ENGAGED AND TENDER TOWARD MY BROTHERS AND SISTERS IN THE FAITH. AND HELP ME CHOOSE TO CONTINUE LOVING. EVEN WHEN IT GETS MESSY AT TIMES. AMEN.

What Are Your Gifts and Talents?

Cheerfully share your home with those who need a meal or a place to stay for the night. God has given each of you some special abilities; be sure to use them to help each other, passing on to others God's many kinds of blessings.

1 PETER 4:9–10 TLB

What a beautiful picture of community. Today's passage reminds us that we're to work collectively as believers. God has equipped each person with different gifts and talents that fit like a puzzle. And when we come together to further the kingdom, we'll be a force for good.

What abilities has God baked into you? Are you great with organizing? Can you speak boldly without fear? Are you a caregiver? Can you write with clarity and passion? Do you have a heart for volunteering your time? Maybe you're a worshipper musically. When you enthusiastically bring your gifts forward, it's an act of love for the Lord and His followers.

LORD, THANK YOU FOR EQUIPPING ME WITH SPECIAL ABILITIES TO SUPPORT THE FURTHERING OF YOUR KINGDOM. GIVE ME THE COURAGE AND CONFIDENCE TO USE THEM. AMEN.

Never Feel Ashamed

If anyone condemns you for following Jesus as the Anointed One, consider yourself blessed. The glorious Spirit of God rests on you.

1 PETER 4:14 VOICE

Don't ever hide your faith because you're worried about being ridiculed. Never feel ashamed for being a believer, for it's the best decision one could ever make. And Peter says we should consider ourselves *blessed* when we face any kind of condemnation for following God. The world simply cannot understand the depth of that decision.

So, offer to pray for someone who is struggling with life. Say a blessing before you eat your meal. Listen to worship music in the car. Read your Bible whenever and wherever you want to. Be bold and opt out of bad behavior rather than give in to peer pressure. Live out your convictions. Friend, God sees the hard choices you make to show Him love, and it delights His heart.

LORD, IT'S A PRIVILEGE TO FOLLOW YOU. I'M SO GRATEFUL TO BE IN YOUR FAMILY. HELP ME KEEP THAT PERSPECTIVE WHEN I FEEL ANY CONDEMNATION FROM THE WORLD. AMEN.

Keep Doing What Is Right

So if you are suffering according to God's will, keep on doing what is right and trust yourself to the God who made you, for he will never fail you.

1 PETER 4:19 TLB

Don't let your own sufferings keep you from being intentional to show love to others. Instead, when hard times hit, let them be what drives you to extend even more compassion. Take the focus off your own mess and direct it toward being kind and generous. Because when you do, it shows God your steadfast faith. It reveals your allegiance. And it keeps you from being self-focused and dismissive of the needs of those around you.

Scripture backs this up when it says to "keep on doing what is right" when we'd rather curl up in a ball and hide under the covers. Keep being thoughtful and considerate. Continue sharing encouragement. Be sympathetic to the hardships others are facing. Have a gentle spirit. Look for ways to help. Be hopeful and spread joy. And when it feels impossible to do, ask God to strengthen you so you can.

LORD, STRENGTHEN ME TO FOCUS ON OTHERS. AMEN.

Be Careful Who You Hang With

Don't hang out with angry people; don't keep company with hotheads. Bad temper is contagious—don't get infected.

PROVERBS 22:24–25 MSG

There is nothing positive or good about surrounding yourself with angry people. Truth is, keeping such company often transfers to you. If you're hanging with happy people, you tend to be happy. If you're hanging with people who value peace, you most likely will too. But if you're hanging out with hotheads and those with a quick temper, it will become part of your operating system in a matter of time.

Since your desire is to love others with a tender heart, be sure you hang out with others who have the same goal. Be mindful of the friends you choose, because they will have great influence over you. . .and you, them. God loves a compassionate heart that seeks to bless others while glorifying Him. Surround yourself with people who feel the same way.

LORD, HELP ME CHOOSE MY FRIENDS WISELY SO THEY REFLECT THE SAME DESIRES I HAVE. GIVE ME DISCERNMENT TO KNOW WHO WILL KEEP MY HEART POINTED IN YOUR DIRECTION. AMEN.

Leaving Them Better

The righteous man is a guide to his neighbor,
but the way of the wicked leads them astray.
PROVERBS 12:26 AMP

What if you decided to leave others better than how you found them? What if your mission was to love them in ways that left them feeling encouraged and blessed? You may not do it perfectly, but think of the difference it could make in someone's day.

How would you walk that out? Maybe you make an effort to connect with your teachers and ask how their week has been. Maybe you offer to help the coach clean up after practice. Maybe you buy a friend her favorite bag of candy. . .just because. Maybe you thank your mom and dad for always being there when you need them. Maybe you invest time in your younger siblings, doing things they enjoy. Regardless, choose to love those around you in ways that guide them toward saving faith in Jesus.

LORD, HELP MY WORDS AND ACTIONS POINT OTHERS TO YOU. LET THEM SEE MY COMPASSION AND KINDNESS AND WANT TO KNOW WHAT MAKES ME DIFFERENT. AMEN.

Forgiving Quickly

He who covers and forgives an offense seeks love, but he who repeats or gossips about a matter separates intimate friends.

PROVERBS 17:9 AMP

One of the kindest things we can do for someone is quickly forgive them. When we choose to extend grace right then and there and move on rather than stay angry, it's an act of love. Being merciful tells the other person they are worth it. It takes the weight of worry off their shoulders. It stops resentment from building between the two of you. And it delights the heart of God.

Choose to lead with love and show compassion when someone messes up. Don't hold a grudge. Don't run to everyone and gossip. Don't sit in it and get stirred up in angst. And don't entertain vengeful thoughts. Instead, take your hurt and anger to God and ask for perspective. Let Him settle your anxious heart. And then lovingly forgive and move on.

LORD, HELP ME MUSTER THE DESIRE TO FORGIVE OTHERS QUICKLY AND FULLY. LET ME CHOOSE TO SHOW THEM LOVE IN SUCH WAYS. AMEN.

Checking Your Alignment

You are adulterers. Don't you know that making friends with this corrupt world order is open aggression toward God? So anyone who aligns with this bogus world system is declaring war against the one true God.

JAMES 4:4 VOICE

Wow. Today's verse is sobering, and it challenges us to check our allegiances. You may want to skip over these powerful words, but don't. Sit with them today and take inventory, asking yourself the tough questions. Have I made friends with the world? Do I invest more into what it offers than what my relationship with God offers? What might need to change?

The Lord wants us to love Him more than we do anything the world has to offer. Sure, it's shiny. It offers temptations, some which feel innocent. There is much fighting for our attention, like the latest and greatest stuff. But scripture says that aligning with this world is aggression toward God. Anything we place above Him fits into this category. Choose today who will get your love and attention.

LORD, LET THE WORLD GROW STRANGELY DIM SO ALL I SEE IS YOU. AMEN.

Praying with a Pure Heart

And when you do ask, you still do not get what you want because your motives are all wrong—because you continually focus on self-indulgence.

James 4:3 voice

When you pray, do so with a pure heart turned toward God. Choose to love Him through prayer by approaching the throne in reverence. Have an attitude of worship. Come to the Lord in fear, meaning with a deep respect for His position. Be in awe of His majesty. And start by thanking God for who He is and how you've seen Him move in your life.

Scripture is clear that when we try to manipulate the Lord as we pray or want to sound more righteous than we are, He's keenly aware. Crying to God with an impure heart and mixed motives almost assures we won't get what we're asking. He won't respond when we focus on self-indulgence.

LORD, LET MY HEART ALWAYS BE FOR YOU AS I PRAY. KNOWING YOUR HEART IS ALWAYS FOR ME. AND LET MY LOVE FOR YOU COME THROUGH IN MY WORDS. AMEN.

Wanting What God Wants

Come close to the one true God, and He will draw close to you. Wash your hands; you have dirtied them in sin. Cleanse your heart, because your mind is split down the middle, your love for God on one side and selfish pursuits on the other.

James 4:8 voice

Truer words have not be spoken. As believers, we're in a constant battle between God's way and ours. We struggle to find balance because we're selfish creatures by nature. And if we don't choose to align our heart with God's heart for us, we will easily justify our self-centered ways every time.

So, how do we love the Lord more? We draw closer to Him. We confess and repent of selfish sins that don't glorify Him. We guard our heart, meaning we protect our thoughts from stinkin' thinkin'. And we invest in our relationship with God through prayer, time in the Word, and time in community with other believers.

LORD, HELP ME LOVE YOU MORE THAN ANYTHING OR ANYONE ELSE. KEEP ME FOCUSED ON WANTING WHAT YOU WANT MOST. AMEN.

You're Not the Judge

My brothers and sisters, do not assault each other with criticism. If you decide your job is to accuse and judge another believer, then you are a self-appointed critic and judge of the law; if so, then you are no longer a doer of the law and subject to its rule; you stand over it as a judge.

JAMES 4:11 VOICE

Today's verse is a great reminder that our job is to simply love. Too often, we decide to be judge and jury, which alienates us from those we care about. We decide to be a self-appointed critic. But friend, if God's Word tells us to stay clear of criticism, then it's a command we should embrace without question.

Sometimes we love by speaking truth. To stay silent as we watch a friend sink into a pit of their own doing isn't showing compassion. But it's important to walk the fine line between accountability and criticism. Ask God to help you understand the difference so you can love with the right motives.

LORD, HELP ME CHOOSE LOVE OVER CRITICISM. AMEN.

Encouraging One Another

What I mean is that we can mutually encourage each other while I am with you. We can be encouraged by the faithfulness we find in each other, both your faithfulness and mine.

ROMANS 1:12 CEB

Have you ever been encouraged by someone's faith? Maybe you watched someone stand strong as their parents walked through a nasty divorce. Maybe you noticed a hopeful attitude in a friend when it seemed every opportunity for a positive outcome disappeared. Maybe you witnessed someone navigating an illness or grief or insecurities, yet they leaned on God at every turn. Or maybe you saw a friend get control of fear rather than allowing it to take them out. Chances are, seeing their faith encouraged yours.

One of the ways we can love others with purpose and passion is by allowing them to see our faith in action. Letting them have insider privileges into what we're battling and sharing how God shows up and settles our spirit are great acts of love. Why? Because it reminds others that He will be there for them too—and there is no greater comfort and hope.

LORD, LET MY FAITH BE ENCOURAGING! AMEN.

Chosen Family

Do not neglect your friend or your parent's friend for that matter. When hard times come, you don't have to travel far to get help from family; a neighbor who is near is better than a brother who is far away.

PROVERBS 27:10 VOICE

Family isn't only the ones related by blood. It can also include those people you've chosen to love. You may consider family to be a broader term that adds in close friends, certain coaches and teachers, kind neighbors, and caring church members. And what makes this expanded *family* so powerful is knowing you're surrounded by those who will help you when needed.

As you go through life, these are the ones you'll lean on. They will be your community—the ones you've elected to love. Your time and heart will invest in this created family, making life sweeter and full of compassion for one another. The reality is that sometimes the most wonderful people in your *family*. . .are those chosen.

LORD, THANK YOU FOR MY COLLECTIVE FAMILY. MAY I LOVE THEM WELL! AMEN.

Comforted by Friends

When Job's three friends heard about all this disaster that had happened to him, they came, each one from his home—Eliphaz from Teman, Bildad from Shuah, and Zophar from Naamah. They agreed to come so they could console and comfort him.

JOB 2:11 CEB

Sometimes what we need more than anything is to be comforted by our friends. We need their encouraging words. We need to know they're on our team, supporting us through the messy moments. We need to feel surrounded by those who think we're worth loving. And when we do, it shifts something in our heart.

To realize we've been handpicked by certain people—chosen to be loved—is a wonderful feeling! Knowing we are valued in such ways helps make us confident and courageous. And every time they show up for us, it deepens our connection. Make sure you are that kind of friend in return. Let others know you chose them too.

LORD, LET ME BE THE KIND OF FRIEND I WANT TO HAVE. HELP ME CHOOSE TO LOVE OTHERS WITH DEEP COMPASSION. AMEN.

How the Heart Reflects

Just as water reflects a person's true face, so the human heart reflects a person's true character.

PROVERBS 27:19 VOICE

Your heart—the collection of your thoughts—shows you what kind of person you are. What you think about and how you treat others reveal your true nature. If you're an angry person who holds on to the past, that's how you'll act. If you are full of insecurity and think little of yourself, it will be reflected in your actions. If you're constantly stressed out and a worrywart, it will be obvious in your responses. None of that will stay hidden.

But at the same time, if your heart is filled to the brim with compassion, it will shine through. The kindness you show your classmates, teammates, and workmates will reveal the goodness inside you. When you return their frustration with thoughtfulness, they will see a tenderness from within. And as you choose to love others with a true genuineness, it will help knit hearts together.

LORD, I WANT WHO I AM ON THE INSIDE TO BE WHO I AM ON THE OUTSIDE. AMEN.

When You're Together

"When two of you get together on anything at all on earth and make a prayer of it, my Father in heaven goes into action. And when two or three of you are together because of me, you can be sure that I'll be there."

MATTHEW 18:19–20 MSG

God loves it when believers gather in community. Something supernatural happens as you pray together, seeking His wisdom and guidance with purpose. That act of togetherness is powerful and catches the attention of God in heaven. And He blesses it.

Letting the Lord be at the center of your relationships opens you up for His goodness to flow in you and through you. It opens you up to commune with the Father in new and fresh ways. And as you embrace His magnificent love in your own life, it allows you to love others with a tender heart. It makes compassion and kindness possible.

LORD, THANK YOU FOR BLESSING COMMUNITY THE WAY YOU DO. THANK YOU FOR HONORING US WHEN WE GET TOGETHER AND PRAY. WHAT A BEAUTIFUL INCENTIVE TO DO LIFE WITH OTHER BELIEVERS. AMEN.

Doing Life with Others

Elijah said to Elisha, "Stay here, because the Lord has sent me to Bethel." But Elisha said, "As the Lord lives and as you live, I won't leave you." So they went down to Bethel.

2 Kings 2:2 CEB

If your goal is to love those around you well, then being willing to walk with them through the ups and downs of life is a must. Just like Elisha did for Elijah, he wanted to be part of what his friend was doing. He cared about the ministry God was asking Elijah to walk out and wanted to stay near in support. Elisha wanted an up-close and personal view of what the Lord was going to do in the prophet's life.

Choosing to do life with others is worth it on so many levels! We get to love in ways that matter most to them, blessing our friends and family with unwavering support. We get to watch how God moves and works in their lives and hearts. And we get to reap the benefits of community with other believers in Christ.

LORD, THANK YOU FOR COMMUNITY! AMEN.

We All Need a Jonathan

After King Saul had finished his conversation with David, David met Jonathan, the king's son, and there was an immediate bond of love between them. Jonathan swore to be his blood brother, and sealed the pact by giving him his robe, sword, bow, and belt.

1 Samuel 18:1–4 TLB

There is something so sweet about a genuine friendship. Having a soul sister (or two) has a wonderful way of making life more fun. It's what keeps you going when things get tough. When you're feeling in the dumps, a good friend can help put a smile back on your face. And when you need to be called higher or challenged to make better decisions, they are the one to hold you accountable.

Do you have a Jonathan in your life today? If so, let them know how much you love and appreciate them. Tell them they matter! If you don't have that special friend, ask God to bring one into your life.

LORD, YOU KNOW MY FRIENDSHIP NEEDS AND WHERE I'M LACKING. HELP ME HAVE A JONATHAN AS WELL AS BE ONE TO SOMEONE ELSE. AMEN.

Loving through Loyalty

Most people claim to be loyal, but can anyone find a trustworthy person?

PROVERBS 20:6 VOICE

The reality is, it's difficult to find someone who is loyal. Why? Because loyalty requires a true focus on selflessness. It involves a divine perspective on loving with a servant's heart. And too often, we're only worried about ourselves. We're faithful to our own needs. And rather than be concerned about being steadfast for others, at critical times we look the other way.

Be the kind of young woman who chooses to love friends with deep devotion, always ready to stand in the gap when help is needed. Show compassion to family by being reliable and dependable no matter what comes up. That kind of consistency brings comfort. It allows them to exhale with relief, knowing they can count on you. And when you show you are dependable in meaningful ways, it speaks volumes to those you care about.

LORD, HELP ME CHOOSE TO LOVE MY FRIENDS AND FAMILY BY BEING TRUSTWORTHY THROUGH THICK AND THIN. LET THEM KNOW ME AS LOYAL. AMEN.

Letting God Carry It All

Cast your burden on the LORD [release it] and He will sustain and uphold you; He will never allow the righteous to be shaken (slip, fall, fail).

PSALM 55:22 AMP

God invites you to dump every burden that's weighing on you, onto Him. When your best friend betrays a secret, or your boyfriend becomes pushy, or your teammate turns into a bully, talk to God about it. When your family is struggling financially or your parents are divorcing, let the Lord hold you up. In those tough seasons of fear and insecurity, release the weight of them into His hands.

Letting God into your life in such ways reveals the truth of your love for Him. That kind of trust requires love to walk it out. And He is clear about wanting to support you in every way. God won't let you down. He won't let you be shaken to the core. And realizing you need Him to get through each day allows this kind of surrendering to happen.

LORD, HERE ARE THE BURDENS I'M CARRYING TODAY. THANK YOU FOR TAKING THEM FROM ME. I TRUST YOU. AMEN.

Your Generosity Is Blessed

Generous people are genuinely blessed
because they share their food with the poor.

PROVERBS 22:9 VOICE

When you spend time with God and let His love infiltrate your heart, generosity with your time and treasure will flow freely from within. You'll want to help the family struggling to make ends meet. You'll look for opportunities to help the homeless. Your heart will bend toward the less fortunate. You'll befriend the new girl. And you will embrace every opportunity to serve, help, and support.

When we choose to love others in meaningful ways, they won't be the only ones blessed. Scripture says the generous will reap a blessing too. That means every time you decide to show compassion, God sees it and responds. He notices your kindheartedness and rewards it. And your thoughtfulness catches His attention, and the Lord's goodness comes your way.

LORD, I WANT TO BE GENEROUS SIMPLY BECAUSE I KNOW IT BLESSES OTHERS. WHILE SCRIPTURE SAYS YOU WILL REWARD ME FOR BEING KIND, IT'S NOT THE DRIVING FORCE FOR MY COMPASSION. I JUST WANT TO FOLLOW YOUR COMMAND TO LOVE. AMEN.

His Company

Stay away from the love of money; be satisfied with what you have. For God has said, "I will never, never fail you nor forsake you."

HEBREWS 13:5 TLB

Don't choose to *love* money. There's nothing wrong with having it, but when we lust for it, we're sinning. We shouldn't be preoccupied with the idea of more and bigger and better. Instead, we should choose to be content with what we have, knowing God will make sure we are cared for in every way. The truth is that nothing in this world has the power to satisfy. . .at least not for long. But having God's presence with us always quenches our thirst.

Friend, do you long for better clothes, a nicer car, more vacations, a bigger home, or more expensive gadgets? Do you crave the latest and greatest? Is retail therapy how you cope with stress and sadness? God wants His company to be your greatest desire because it delivers the greatest satisfaction.

LORD, HELP ME WANT YOU OVER ANYTHING THE WORLD CAN OFFER. LET ME CHOOSE TO SEEK YOUR PRESENCE EVERY TIME. AMEN.

Entertaining Angels

Continue to love each other with true brotherly love. Don't forget to be kind to strangers, for some who have done this have entertained angels without realizing it!

HEBREWS 13:1–2 TLB

This is a fun, yet serious, warning. Imagine the fact there are some who have encountered angels without knowing it. Their lives have intersected with the heavenlies. This is a powerful reminder for us to always show compassion and kindness. Since we may never know who we'll meet, it's important to be on our best behavior. That means we should respond to everyone as if they are divine messengers.

Friend, if your heart is in the right place, choosing to love those around you isn't difficult. It just takes a little intentionality and an active faith. It's deciding to be thoughtful and selfless. It's having a servant's heart.

LORD, IT'S EXCITING TO THINK I COULD ENCOUNTER AN ANGEL HERE ON EARTH. HELP ME KEEP THAT MIND-SET SO I TREAT OTHERS WITH A GENTLE SPIRIT. AMEN.

Loving Others in Desperation

I knew, when I saw Doeg the Edomite that day, that he would certainly tell Saul. I am responsible for the death of every person in your family. Stay here with me, and don't be afraid. The one who seeks my life also seeks yours; you will certainly be safe with me.

1 SAMUEL 22:22–23 VOICE

When Abiathar fled to David as the only survivor of King Saul's massacre at Nob, he was promised protection. David, the future king, chose to love this man. And his loyalty eventually paid off as he was made high priest when David was throned. Abiathar was offered a safe place from his fear. He was given shelter from Saul's vengeance.

We can choose to love others who are in desperate situations too. We can stand with someone against a bully. We can be with them as they have hard conversations. And we can help them advocate for themselves in unfair situations.

Be available to those who need help. Let them know you're a safe place in tough times.

LORD, OPEN MY HEART TO STAND WITH THOSE WHO NEED TO FEEL SAFE AND SECURE IN CHALLENGING MOMENTS. AMEN.

Being God's Friend

The faith in his heart was made known in his behavior. In fact, his commitment was perfected by his obedience. That's what Scripture means when it says, "Abraham entrusted himself to God, and God credited him with righteousness." And living a faithful life earned Abraham the title of "God's friend."

JAMES 2:22–23 VOICE

What does it mean when today's scripture says, "The faith in his heart was made known in his behavior"? Consider that Abraham made a commitment to not only love God with his whole heart but also with his life choices. He obeyed the Lord's commands with purpose and passion. And at every crossroads of his flesh and God's will, Abraham chose God, earning him the title of His friend. Simply amazing.

You have the chance to love the Lord in the same ways. It's not a matter of being perfect but of being intentional. Pledge to love Him with your heart, soul, and mind. Ask for wisdom, listen for His leading, and then follow God's ways. Be God's friend too.

LORD, I WANT MY HEART FOR YOU TO BE AS STEADFAST AS ABRAHAM'S. I WANT TO BE YOUR FRIEND. AMEN.

The Danger of Favoritism

Dear brothers, how can you claim
that you belong to the Lord Jesus Christ,
the Lord of glory, if you show favoritism to
rich people and look down on poor people?

JAMES 2:1 TLB

Because the Lord never shows favoritism, neither should we. There shouldn't be one group of people we like over another. How much money they do or do not have shouldn't matter. Where they live, the car they drive, the position they play on the team, or the grades they make aren't factors we need to consider. It's a form of prejudice.

But the truth is that we may connect better with some over others. We may have more in common with certain people and like hanging out with them instead. We were made for community, and there's nothing wrong with that. Today's verse is reminding us, however, to not sit in judgment. It's not our job. We're to love those around us and leave discrimination out of our heart.

LORD, HELP ME NOT BE PREJUDICED AND JUDGMENTAL TOWARD OTHERS. LET THE ONLY FAVORITISM I SHOW BE TOWARD YOU. AMEN.

Blessed in Return

For there will be no mercy to those who have shown no mercy. But if you have been merciful, then God's mercy toward you will win out over his judgment against you.

JAMES 2:13 TLB

When you choose to love others through kindness and generosity, it will come back to you. Every time you're sympathetic, you'll experience it too. And when you decide to extend grace and mercy, you will be blessed by it. This isn't just an idea or playbook to follow, this truth is backed up by scripture.

Knowing God promises to bless your obedience, give Him the chance to prove it. Love others well, showing compassion at every opportunity. Decide to listen to them to gain better understanding into their needs and desires. Be a gift to those around you, always quick to help in any way you can. Live each day with a servant's heart and watch for the ways God blesses you in return.

LORD, OPEN MY EYES AND MY HEART TO THE WAYS I CAN SHOW MERCY TO OTHERS. AMEN.

When Words and Actions Align

Brothers and sisters, it doesn't make any sense to say you have faith and act in a way that denies that faith. Mere talk never gets you very far, and a commitment to Jesus only in words will not save you.

JAMES 2:14 VOICE

Today's verse is a call to make sure what you say and what you do align. Not only should a declaration of faith be revealed in both your words and actions but also in how you choose to treat others. It's not enough to say you love someone if you're going to treat them like dirt. To say you care for their feelings but then beat them up verbally is destabilizing. And telling someone they're valuable to you but then giving them no time or attention is confusing. So be intentional with walking out what your mouth says.

When you say faith is important but then treat others in such reckless ways, let it be a red flag. And ask God to realign your heart with His.

LORD, LET MY WORDS AND ACTIONS ALIGN WITH NOT ONLY OTHERS BUT ALSO WITH YOU. AMEN.

The Beauty of Loyalty

But Ruth said, "Don't force me to leave you; don't make me go home. Where you go, I go; and where you live, I'll live. Your people are my people, your God is my god; where you die, I'll die, and that's where I'll be buried, so help me God— not even death itself is going to come between us!"

RUTH 1:16–17 MSG

There's something beautiful about loyalty. Maybe you have a best friend who always has your back. Maybe the relationship with your parents is so strong that you never doubt their support, even when you make mistakes. Maybe you have a special bond with a teacher or a coach who stands by you through thick and thin. And maybe you're that dependable and devoted person to others as well.

In today's passage of scripture, Ruth gives us a powerful example of loyalty, and it's heartwarming. God chose to include it in His Word for a reason. So, let her steadfastness be an example of how to love others well. Be that constant source of support to your friends and family, faithful through it all.

LORD, LET ME CHOOSE TO LOVE IN SUCH WAYS. AMEN.

Shutting Down the Gossip

He who goes about as a gossip reveals secrets, but he who is trustworthy and faithful keeps a matter hidden.

Proverbs 11:13 AMP

There's nothing good about gossip. And every time we hear something negative and share it, we aren't choosing to love. Instead, we have decided it's our place to let more people know information that's hurtful and maybe even untrue.

We are called higher as believers. God commands that we love one another, protecting and defending as needed. Spreading the latest news—especially when it's juicy—is disobedience, plain and simple. It's choosing to not love that person, displeasing the Lord by your actions. Be the kind of young woman who is trustworthy with sensitive information. When scandalous news comes your way, be faithful to shut it down. You may be at odds with the person in the center of the gossip but showing your integrity in that moment will bring blessings into your life in ways you cannot imagine.

LORD, CREATE IN ME A HEART THAT LONGS TO PROTECT AND ALWAYS DEFENDS. AMEN.

Peaceful Places

How good and pleasant it is when brothers and sisters live together in peace!

PSALM 133:1 VOICE

The world is crazy these days! It tells us that what's right is wrong, and what's wrong is now right. And the complete insanity being produced and pushed in today's society is unbelievable. And while we're not *of* the world, we are *in* the world and having to navigate foolishness all around. Knowing that, take seriously the encouragement in the verse above.

It's important we find places that are good and pleasant—places where we can experience a sense of calmness. We need moments to breathe in goodness and exhale the multitude of stressors that plague us. And when we surround ourselves with godly friends and family, it's possible. We'll be able to experience peace even when school is difficult, work is overwhelming, people are mean-spirited, and we're bogged down by fear and worry. By faith, we'll be able to live peacefully together, strengthening us for each new day.

LORD, HELP ME HELP CREATE PEACEFUL LIVING WITH THOSE AROUND ME. AMEN.

Helping Back on the Right Path

Dear brothers, if a Christian is overcome by some sin, you who are godly should gently and humbly help him back onto the right path, remembering that next time it might be one of you who is in the wrong.

GALATIANS 6:1 TLB

When you take the time and energy to help someone who is tangled in sinful activity, you're choosing to love them. They may not appreciate that you pointed out their trespasses. They probably won't like being called out, even lovingly. And they may even be angry that you discovered their wrongdoing in the first place. But being part of a community of believers requires holding one another accountable.

Ask God to give you the right words when you talk to your friend about her dangerous choices. Let Him fill you with tenderness as you confront your teammate or classmate about their reckless behavior. And be ready for the times others come to you with much-needed redirection. We're all in this together.

LORD, IT'S A PRIVILEGE AND A BURDEN TO LIVE IN COMMUNITY. LET ME LOVE OTHERS BY BEING WILLING TO HELP THEM BACK ON THE RIGHT PATH. AMEN.

Don't Be a Fool

Share each other's troubles and problems, and so obey our Lord's command. If anyone thinks he is too great to stoop to this, he is fooling himself. He is really a nobody.

GALATIANS 6:2–3 TLB

God wants us to be a good friend to those around us. He wants us to love our family in meaningful ways. His plan for our life is to thrive in community, being willing and able to step in and support one another. We're to work together for solutions, sharing the load of each other's troubles and problems. And when we choose to love in such ways, God is glorified.

The problem is that sometimes we think we're too lofty to help. We feel inconvenienced when asked to offer support. That kind of attitude is ugly and ungodly. It's foolish. And God isn't impressed. Instead, be quick to love others well. Ask Him to open your heart to those around you.

LORD, GIVE ME A WILLINGNESS TO SHARE THE TROUBLES AND PROBLEMS OF THOSE AROUND ME. LET ME ALWAYS BE WILLING TO LEND A HAND TO THOSE IN NEED. AMEN.

Kindness Brings Blessings

And let us not get tired of doing what is right, for after a while we will reap a harvest of blessing if we don't get discouraged and give up. That's why whenever we can we should always be kind to everyone, and especially to our Christian brothers.

GALATIANS 6:9–10 TLB

Today's verse makes an interesting connection between being kind and not giving up in discouragement. It suggests that when we choose to love, it has the potential to shift our outlook. Maybe it's because when we're tenderhearted, it puts us in a good mood. We see the goodness in the world, and it's encouraging. Maybe it helps to create a hopeful attitude that everything will work out for the best. Regardless of the why, there's a benefit to kindness we can't miss.

Let love be what guides you, especially with other believers. And in return, watch as your compassion enables you to stay the course and receive the blessing. It's a win-win.

LORD, WHEN I'M FEELING WEARY. REMIND ME TO SEEK OUT WAYS TO BE KIND SO WE'RE ALL ENCOURAGED TO STAND STRONG. AMEN.

Loving God More

As for me, God forbid that I should boast about anything except the cross of our Lord Jesus Christ. Because of that cross, my interest in all the attractive things of the world was killed long ago, and the world's interest in me is also long dead.

GALATIANS 6:14 TLB

When you become a believer—recognizing Jesus as God's Son who died on the cross for your sins and rose three days later—the things of this world will lose their glitter and glow. Your heart will choose to be focused on eternal treasures rather than worldly ones. Your cravings for the latest trends will diminish as your desire to follow God's ways grows more important.

Take inventory of your heart's focus today. Are you more absorbed by what the world can offer or what God promises to provide? Is your attention pointed toward the latest and greatest here on earth, or are you longing for more of Jesus? Be the kind of young woman who chooses to love the Lord with all your heart, mind, and soul.

LORD, HELP ME LOVE YOU MORE THAN ANYTHING THIS WORLD HAS TO OFFER. AMEN.

Just Showing Up

So they sat down on the ground with Job for seven days and seven nights and no one spoke a word to him, for they saw that his pain was very great.

JOB 2:13 AMP

What wonderful friends! When Eliphaz the Temanite, Bildad the Shuhite, and Zophar the Naamathite heard about the extraordinary losses their friend had suffered, they packed up and headed to Job's home. Rather than mail a card, make a call, or send a text message, they knew their presence was necessary. They chose to love Job not only in the good times but also in the tough times.

Sometimes all we can do for our friends is show up. We may not have the perfect words that will heal their hearts. We won't be able to fix their circumstances and remove their pain, because we're not their savior. But we can be available. We can cry with them, sharing in their sufferings. And when we do, they will know we love them deeply.

LORD, GIVE ME THE COURAGE TO SHOW UP FOR MY FRIENDS AND LOVE THEM WITH MY PRESENCE. AMEN.

Embracing Counsel, Instruction, and Correction

Listen to counsel, receive instruction, and accept correction, that you may be wise in the time to come.

PROVERBS 19:20 AMP

Sometimes it's so hard to handle criticism. Even if constructive, no one likes to hear they're doing things wrong. We don't want to be told our best isn't good enough or our efforts are misguided. And if we had it our way, chances are we'd want to be told how wonderful we are instead. Amen? But how does that truly benefit us?

Today, ask God to give you a change of heart so you can receive correction and see the love in it. When a parent calls out a misconception, or a coach suggests a different approach, or a friend points out a mistake, embrace it. Chances are it's because they care for you deeply and want what is best. So, welcome their counsel, instruction, and correction. And let God use it to make you wise!

LORD, HELP ME REMEMBER THAT OTHERS OFTEN SHOW LOVE THROUGH CONSTRUCTIVE CRITICISM. GIVE ME THE ABILITY TO EMBRACE WHAT I NEED TO HEAR AND THE DISCERNMENT TO RELEASE WHAT I DON'T. AMEN.

The Benefits of Good Choices

When people make good choices,
He is pleased; He even causes their
enemies to live peacefully near them.
PROVERBS 16:7 VOICE

Have you ever considered that when you make good choices, they have far-reaching benefits? When you honor your parents by obeying, when you study for the test rather than cheating, and when you stand up for truth, it pleases the Lord. Every time you choose to be patient rather than annoyed by your siblings, God takes notice. Showing integrity when working or volunteering thrills His heart. And deciding to surround yourself with like-minded friends who respect rules and love the Lord delights His heart to no end. But even more than that, your good choices lead to peaceful lives. Scripture says He will honor your pursuit of smart living by causing your enemies to be more agreeable.

Being blessed for obedience is a powerful theme knitted throughout scripture. Let it be a driving force every day.

LORD, THANK YOU FOR REWARDING ME WITH THE GIFT OF PEACE WHEN I MAKE GOOD CHOICES. AMEN.

When They Cross Your Mind

Whenever you cross my mind, I thank my God for you and for the gift of knowing you. My spirit is lightened with joy whenever I pray for you (and I do constantly).

PHILIPPIANS 1:3–4 VOICE

One of the ways we can choose to love others is by praying for them when prompted by God. Just like Paul mentions in today's verse, every time someone comes across your mind. . .pray. You may not know what kinds of prayers they need, but you can ask God to meet them in their situation. You can ask Him to be big in their circumstances. You can ask the Lord to give them what they need in that very moment. You can ask Him to provide wisdom, peace, joy, discernment, and perseverance.

It's a burden and privilege to pray for those around you. And as believers, prayer is the most powerful weapon we have, because it works. So wield that weapon with precision, choosing to lift someone up in the name of Jesus whenever they come to mind.

LORD, THANK YOU FOR PLACING PEOPLE ON MY HEART SO I CAN LOVE THEM THROUGH PRAYER. AMEN.

Instilling Courage in Others

My imprisonment has instilled courage in most of our brothers and sisters, so they are trusting God more and have been even more daring as they speak the good news without fear.

PHILIPPIANS 1:14 VOICE

When you choose to love the Lord regardless of what's happening in your life, it speaks volumes. Each time you stand strong in faith—whether in good times or bad—it helps instill courage in others. There's something powerful about watching the faithful endure difficult times without crumbling. Seeing them survive discouragement, withstand disappointment, and overcome failure with God's help builds confidence He will help all His children.

And if you think about it, living faith out loud is not only choosing to love God but also those around you too. It's caring enough to show them how to experience the ups and downs of life through a steadfast relationship with the Lord.

LORD, GIVE ME THE FAITH TO LIVE IN SUCH A WAY THAT MY LIFE POINTS TO YOU NO MATTER WHAT I'M FACING. IN GOOD TIMES AND BAD. LET ME LOVE OTHERS BY SHOWING THEM YOU. AMEN.

Steadfast Faith

Don't be paralyzed in any way by what your opponents are doing. Your steadfast faith in the face of opposition is a sign that they are doomed and that you have been graced with God's salvation.

PHILIPPIANS 1:28 VOICE

Choose to stay close to God every day but especially when you're facing mean-spirited people who want to hurt you. Don't let the school bully paralyze or discourage you. Don't let the trash-talking teammate intimidate you. And don't allow the mean girls to make you question your value and worth. Instead, hold fast to your faith and lean on the Lord. Let Him settle your spirit and steady your heart. And from that place, let God keep your heart tender so you can choose to love rather than give way to bitterness.

Each time your faith wins out, be encouraged. It reveals the depth of your relationship with the Lord. And it keeps you blameless in His eyes.

LORD, LET MY FAITH RISE UP WHEN I FACE OPPOSITION. HELP ME ALWAYS RESPOND WITH CONFIDENCE, KNOWING YOU ARE WITH ME. AND WITH YOUR HELP, LET ME CHOOSE TO LOVE OTHERS, EVEN WHEN THEY'RE UNKIND. AMEN.

The Gift of Friendship

Jonathan repeated his pledge of love and friendship for David. He loved David more than his own soul!

1 SAMUEL 20:17 MSG

Today's scripture reveals the powerful friendship between David and Jonathan. God had knitted their hearts together, allowing for a deep devotion toward each other. They were the real deal, true-blue buddies. And these two showed robust compassion, so much so they cared for each other more than their own selves. Pretty amazing, wouldn't you say?

God is delighted when we choose to love in such ways. Because He made us for community, every time we choose to love selflessly, it's noted in the heavens. The Lord sees it when we extend great kindness. He sees our generous spirit. And each time we're gentle and caring toward another—fulfilling the command to love others—blessings will follow. Choosing to love out of obedience doesn't go unnoticed.

LORD, THANK YOU FOR THE EXAMPLE OF SACRIFICIAL FRIENDSHIP IN YOUR WORD. LET ME PURSUE THIS KIND OF LOVE WITH ENTHUSIASM. TEACH ME HOW TO CARE FOR OTHERS WITH SUCH PURPOSE. HELP ME CHOOSE TO LOVE MY FRIENDS WITH THIS KIND OF PASSION. AMEN.

Being Straightforward

Don't walk around with a chip on your shoulder, always spoiling for a fight. Don't try to be like those who shoulder their way through life. Why be a bully? "Why not?" you say. Because God can't stand twisted souls. It's the straightforward who get his respect.

Proverbs 3:30–32 msg

So many of us try to navigate life alone. Maybe it's because we think we know what's best for ourselves. Maybe it's because we've been burned in the past and struggle to trust the motives of others. Maybe it's a pride issue. Maybe it's rooted in deep insecurity. Regardless, God loves it when we're humble and honest with Him.

Scripture encourages us to create a straightforward relationship with the Lord. The idea is to love Him, choosing to be up front and sincere rather than acting like we have it all together. You can trust God with your heart.

LORD, HELP ME BE HUMBLE WITH YOU AND MY COMMUNITY. HELP ME OPEN UP WITH EVERY STRUGGLE, BEING CANDID ABOUT MY WORRIES. AND HELP ME BE GENTLE WITH OTHERS, NOT ROUGH. HELP ME CHOOSE LOVE EVERY TIME. AMEN.

No One but God

For all my wanting, I don't have anyone but You in heaven. There is nothing on earth that I desire other than You. I admit how broken I am in body and spirit, but God is my strength, and He will be mine forever.

PSALM 73:25–26 VOICE

Sometimes we get to desperate places where we realize God is all we have. Our friends may try to help, but they can't change the tough road we're having to walk. We have family who dearly love us, but they can't fix the brokenness we feel. And as much as we want someone or something to make us feel better, the only one who can is God.

Ask Him to make you aware of His love. Let Him soothe your broken heart, instill courage, embolden resolve, lessen fear, or untangle insecurities. Your mess doesn't intimidate Him. Instead, He wants to show you great compassion and kindness. Choose to let God be who meets you in the moment, willing and able to restore your heart, mind, and soul.

LORD, YOU ARE ALL I NEED. AND I LOVE YOU FOR LOVING ME. I WILL ALWAYS CHOOSE YOU! AMEN.

Telling Everyone

But the closer I am to You, my God, the better because life with You is good. O Lord, the Eternal, You keep me safe—I will tell everyone what You have done.

PSALM 73:28 VOICE

Don't keep God's goodness in your life a secret. Be ready and willing to share what He's done because it's a huge encouragement to those struggling. You know firsthand the difference it makes when you stay close to God through hard times. You understand how following His will and ways brings hope. You see how life is better with Him in the mix.

So, friend, when the opportunity presents itself, share how He's saved you. Talk about the ways God has comforted and strengthened you in those tough moments. And recognize it as an act of love when you remind friends and family about the Lord's strength and compassion. You are pointing them to the one who can meet every need.

LORD, GIVE ME COURAGE TO SHOW COMPASSION TO THOSE AROUND ME BY SHARING THE GOOD THINGS YOU HAVE DONE. LET ME LOVINGLY POINT THEM TO YOU FOR HELP AND HOPE. AMEN.

When You Feel Abandoned

When it was time for my first defense, no one showed up to support me. Everyone abandoned me (may it not be held against them) except the Lord.

2 TIMOTHY 4:16–17 VOICE

Few things feel worse than being abandoned in a time of need. We expect a parent to fight for us or a best friend to stand up in our defense. We assume a teacher will advocate or clear up a misunderstanding. We anticipate a small group leader will stand in the gap. So, when we're left alone and those we felt would come through don't, it leaves us with a deep wound of feeling unloved and unvalued.

But, friend, you can choose to love those around you in meaningful ways. Because you've experienced rejection, you are now an expert on how to make those around you feel known and seen. You understand the importance of showing up. And you can remind them that while others may have abandoned them in their pain, God never will.

LORD, HELP ME LOVE OTHERS THROUGH COMPANIONSHIP AND POINTING THEM TO YOUR UNSHAKABLE FAITHFULNESS. AMEN.

The Gift of Divine Peace

"I am leaving you with a gift—peace of mind and heart! And the peace I give isn't fragile like the peace the world gives. So don't be troubled or afraid."

JOHN 14:27 TLB

God loves you so much that He created a divine peace you can access at any time. Knowing the flimsy and brittle solutions the world touts, God made His peace so wonderful and amazing that it can't compare. It's a gift for every believer to grab hold of when life gets hairy.

When your friend group is struggling, or your grades are failing, or your family is going through a hard time, or your self-worth is under attack, don't sit in despair. The Lord doesn't want you to be stressed or anxious, always worried things won't work out. Instead, He is inviting you into His perfect peace that will steady your heart and settle your mind. What a blessing to serve a God who chooses to love in such a wonderful way.

LORD, THANK YOU FOR GIVING ME ACCESS TO DIVINE PEACE THAT IS STURDY IN THE HARDEST OF TIMES. AMEN.

The Problem with Persistent Sin

The ones who live in an intimate relationship with Him do not persist in sin, but anyone who persists in sin has not seen and does not know the real Jesus. Children, don't let anyone pull one over on you. The one doing the right thing is just imitating Jesus, the Righteous One.

1 JOHN 3:6–7 VOICE

This is a sobering passage of scripture designed to make you self-evaluate your faith walk. It challenges you to take a look at how you're living day to day, both in the words you speak and the actions you take. And it causes you to examine the ways you're interacting with God and others. By design, He uses all of these to draw you closer and reveal truth.

Friend, are you living in habitual sin? Are there things you're allowing in your life that do not glorify the Lord? Do you know what the Bible says but refuse to follow it? Being in an intimate relationship with God—choosing to love Him with your heart, mind, and soul—cannot coexist with persistent sin.

LORD, HELP MY FAITH BE AUTHENTIC IN EVERY WAY. AMEN.

Forgiving One Another

Instead, be kind to each other, tenderhearted, forgiving one another, just as God has forgiven you because you belong to Christ.

EPHESIANS 4:32 TLB

Choosing to love sounds simple, but we know from experience it is not. Even with every great intention, we fall short from time to time. We may love someone dearly, but they end up the victim of collateral damage from our bad day at school, at practice, or at work. All our frustration—none of which they created—comes out at them in hurtful ways. And truth be told, we've also been on the receiving end of this too. God knew this would be part of the human condition, which is why He talks so much about forgiveness.

Let's choose to extend grace, even when it sets us off and we feel unforgiving. Let's ask God to give perspective so we can see what's really going on. Because when we choose to love no matter what, it means just that. We are committed to loving family and friends by keeping short accounts of wrongs and living unoffended.

LORD, HELP ME BE QUICK TO FORGIVE JUST AS YOU HAVE FORGIVEN ME! AMEN.

Bad Behavior

Stop being mean, bad-tempered, and angry.
Quarreling, harsh words, and dislike of others
should have no place in your lives.

EPHESIANS 4:31 TLB

Scripture is very clear about what bad behavior we're to avoid, knowing it does nothing to create community with others. It may feel good in the moment. In our opinion, people may rightly deserve a healthy dose of our temper. Harsh words may come easily and quickly. But as a Christ follower, they have no place in our lives.

If the goal is to always choose love, then chewing someone out takes us in the opposite direction. How can we love when we deeply dislike someone? Can we proclaim a desire to live with compassion when we're always fighting and bickering, trying to get our own way at all costs? How can we justify being mean at the same time touting our faith? We can't. We have to let God tender our hearts and smooth the rough edges so love flows effortlessly.

LORD, HELP ME LOVE OTHERS IN WAYS THAT BLESS THEM AND GLORIFY YOU. AND HELP ANY BAD BEHAVIOR STAY IN THE PAST. I DON'T WANT IT TO BE PART OF MY LIFE ANY LONGER. AMEN.

Learning to Comfort Others

He's the one who comforts us in all our trouble so that we can comfort other people who are in every kind of trouble. We offer the same comfort that we ourselves received from God.

2 CORINTHIANS 1:4 CEB

One of the most wonderful things God does for us is provide the gift of comfort. Not only does it calm our spirit and reignite hope, but it also gives us the skills to be a comfort to others. He has a dual purpose in it. In God's unshakable encouragement and compassion, He teaches us how to meet the emotional needs of those around us. We learn how to love friends and family with purpose and intentionality. What an amazing God!

Rather than have self-pity for the difficulties you'll face, recognize them as training opportunities. The Lord will meet you in those messy moments, comfort your heart, and show you how to help others when they struggle. You'll be fully equipped to choose love.

LORD, I'M ALWAYS AMAZED BY HOW YOU WORK IN MY LIFE SO I'M ABLE TO HELP OTHERS WORK THROUGH THEIRS. THANK YOU FOR BEING YOU! AMEN.

One Big Happy Family

And now this word to all of you: You should be like one big happy family, full of sympathy toward each other, loving one another with tender hearts and humble minds.

1 PETER 3:8 TLB

God's command for community is found all throughout His Word. Countless times we're told about the power of it. We read the ways we can begin to thrive in it. The Bible clearly shares the dos and don'ts surrounding it. In fact, today's verse encourages us to be one big happy family! So how do we do that God's way?

Scripture tells us to be full of sympathy, which is to be compassionate and kind. We're to consider the feelings of others above our own. We're to strive to understand one another and be willing to listen rather than just talk. God wants us to have tender hearts that care for the burdens of others and humble minds so we don't think ourselves better than anyone else. Simply stated, we're to choose to love those around us with a servant's heart.

LORD, HELP ME LOVE AND SUPPORT MY BELIEVING FAMILY WELL! AMEN.

A Promise for Kindness

Don't repay evil for evil. Don't snap back at those who say unkind things about you. Instead, pray for God's help for them, for we are to be kind to others, and God will bless us for it.

1 PETER 3:9 TLB

There is a beautiful blessing promised when we choose to be kind. Every time we extend grace rather than deliver revenge, it's noted in the heavens. When we keep our mouths shut and don't spew the snarky remarks in response, the Lord takes notice. God is delighted when we don't live offended by every little thing and instead choose joy. His hope and expectation are that we choose to love others with our words and actions. And with the Lord's help, we can absolutely do it.

Where do you need His help with this today? Who are you struggling to love? Is it a certain friend, a younger sibling, a school bully, a faculty member, or a prideful teammate? Ask God to fill your heart with compassion and give you the grit to choose love.

LORD, YOU KNOW MY STRUGGLES AND JUST WHAT I NEED TO OVERCOME THEM. PLEASE HELP ME. AMEN.

Peaceful Living

If you want a happy, good life, keep control of your tongue, and guard your lips from telling lies. Turn away from evil and do good. Try to live in peace even if you must run after it to catch and hold it!

1 PETER 3:10–11 TLB

When God highlights peaceful living in His Word, take it to heart. It matters greatly to Him because it's what helps make community strong. He values that connection between believers, and much of the Bible tells us how to love effectively so we can work together to share the gospel. The truth is we need friends and family, and they need us.

Today's passage gives commonsense ways to love, which is good because we often need reminders. Let's heed the command to watch what we say, because our words can deeply hurt. Let's be truth tellers, staying away from lies that can cause trouble. Let's choose good over evil so we can live at peace with those around us. In doing so, we're choosing to love, and it pleases His heart.

LORD, HELP ME LIVE A GOOD LIFE
AND LOVE OTHERS WELL. AMEN.

Defending Your Hope

But exalt Him as Lord in your heart. Always be ready to offer a defense, humbly and respectfully, when someone asks why you live in hope. Keep your conscience clear so that those who ridicule your good conduct in the Anointed and say bad things about you will be put to shame.

1 PETER 3:15–16 VOICE

As a Christ follower, there's no good reason to be without hope. When a friendship crumbles, when we fail a class, when we don't make the team, when we disappoint a parent, when we make a bad choice, when we are fired from a job, there is still hope we can cling to. Others may not understand why you're wearing a smile with a peaceful heart, so be ready to share your faith! Tell them about being forgiven. Tell them about God's unconditional love. Tell them God doesn't expect perfection.

And if you're ridiculed for being peaceful in the midst of a problem, let it go. Give the Lord glory for strengthening you through the storm and choose to love anyway. Who knows—maybe your testimony will lead them to God!

LORD, THANK YOU FOR HOPE. AMEN.

Motives Check

If a person owns the kinds of things we need to make it in the world but refuses to share with those in need, is it even possible that God's love lives in him?

1 John 3:17 voice

Today's scripture poses a great thought because it challenges us to check our motives. It makes us ask the question, "Do our words and actions line up?" Think about it for a minute. When we say we're someone's friend, are we willing to hold them up in hard times? Would we go to extraordinary measures to back up our declaration of love? When we tell them to call if we can help, do we meet their need when they do? Are we willing to share our time and resources?

When you become a believer, a heart change takes place. There's a transformation process that begins to slowly shift your heart and mind toward community. And the Holy Spirit begins His work in your life, helping you find the desire to choose love over selfishness.

LORD, LET YOUR LOVE BE EVIDENT IN HOW I LIVE MY LIFE AND TREAT OTHERS. AMEN.

That Pesky Critical Spirit

"Don't pick on people, jump on their failures, criticize their faults—unless, of course, you want the same treatment. That critical spirit has a way of boomeranging."

MATTHEW 7:1–2 MSG

Today's verses give us a wonderful and powerful warning. And honestly, the chances are good that we need these kinds of reminders from time to time. Why? Because it's easy to start picking on people, especially when we're already annoyed. Pointing out shortcomings and being critical often come quickly. And if we're not careful, we can feel at home sitting in the judgment seat. But is that the treatment we want in return? Probably not.

So instead of falling into old, familiar patterns, let's be more aware of how we're acting toward others. Let's encourage with our words and affirm with our deeds. Let's point out the good things and let any failures go. Let's choose to love, not give in to a critical spirit.

LORD, MAKE ME AWARE OF THE TIMES I'M BEING NITPICKY. LET ME KNOW WHEN I'M TREATING OTHERS IN HURTFUL WAYS. AND PLEASE REMOVE EVERY FAULT-FINDING TENDENCY IN ME. AMEN.

Do Unto Others

This is what our Scriptures come to teach: in everything, in every circumstance, do to others as you would have them do to you.

MATTHEW 7:12 VOICE

This is a key concept in the Bible, the idea that we're to treat others how we want to be treated. That means if we want to be forgiven when we mess up, then we should be quick to forgive. If we want good, loyal friends, then we should act the same. If our desire is for compassion in hard times, let's be quick to offer it to others. And if we want to be loved fully and completely—not having our shortcomings held against us—then we should love this way for friends and family too.

When we choose to do to others as we want them to do to us, it helps develop an understanding of important ways to love with purpose. It helps us prioritize how we interact, knowing the impact it may have. And it deepens our connection to others because we're both choosing to love one another!

LORD, HELP ME BE INTENTIONAL TO TREAT OTHERS THE WAY I WANT TO BE TREATED IN RETURN. AMEN.

Open Arms

"So he returned home to his father. And while he was still a long distance away, his father saw him coming, and was filled with loving pity and ran and embraced him and kissed him."

LUKE 15:20 TLB

If you remember the story, this son had asked for his portion of inheritance early and blew through it fast and furious. And once broke, he returned home in desperation and shame. It would have made sense for his father to reject him. Who would've blamed him for sending his son away in anger? But that's not what happened. Instead, the father chose love without a thought. He ran to the son and embraced him. What a powerful example to follow in our own lives today.

With God's help, we can extend the same kindness to the undeserving. We can choose to overlook every offense and open our arms in love. Rather than respond in anger, hurt, or annoyance, we can extend grace. Let God tender your heart and fill it with compassion in the right moments.

LORD, THIS FEELS SO HARD TO DO! HELP ME CHOOSE LOVE WHEN MY HEART IS STRUGGLING. AMEN.

Caring for the Poor

Whoever cares for the poor makes a loan to the Eternal; such kindness will be repaid in full and with interest.

PROVERBS 19:17 VOICE

What are some practical ways you can care for the poor? Maybe you bring a warm meal to the beggar on the street. Maybe you donate your unused clothes and shoes to an organization who serves that people group. Maybe you volunteer your time or financially support a local shelter. Maybe you share encouragement, offer to pray, or sit with someone to show they matter. Regardless of the way, God expects us to be His hands and feet and will bless those who put forth such effort.

Ask Him to open your eyes so you can see people in need. Let Him know you're ready and willing to love those around you in meaningful ways. It's easy to walk through this life without noticing the needs around you. We can often be self-absorbed. So, be intentional to look for opportunities and be ready to respond with compassion.

LORD, FORGIVE ME FOR THE TIMES I DIDN'T CHOOSE TO LOVE THE POOR. HELP ME TO NOT MAKE THAT MISTAKE AGAIN. AMEN.

About the Author

Carey Scott is an author, speaker, and certified Biblical Life Coach who's honest about her walk with the Lord—stumbles, fumbles, and all. With authenticity and humor, she challenges women to be real, not perfect, and reminds them to trust God as their Source above all else. Carey lives in Colorado and is surrounded by a wonderful family and group of friends who keep her motivated, real, and humble. You can find her at CareyScott.org.